W9-AWO-585

10
Is the Death Penalty Just?

Carla Mooney

INCONTROVERSY

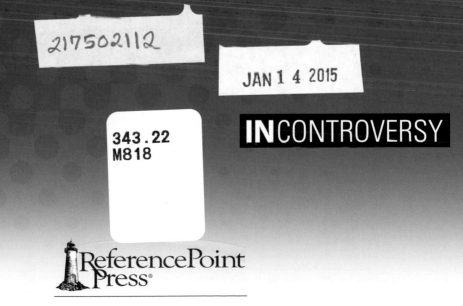

ReferencePoint
Press®

San Diego, CA

ReferencePoint
Press®

© 2015 ReferencePoint Press, Inc.
Printed in the United States

For more information, contact:
ReferencePoint Press, Inc.
PO Box 27779
San Diego, CA 92198
www. ReferencePointPress.com

LIBRARY OF CONGRESS CATALOGING-IN-PUBLICATION DATA

Mooney, Carla, 1970–
  Is the death penalty just? / by Carla Mooney.
    pages cm. -- (In controversy series)
  Includes bibliographical references and index.
   ISBN 978-1-60152-714-1 (hardback) -- ISBN 1-60152-714-4 (hardback)
 1. Capital punishment--United States--Juvenile literature. 2. Criminal justice, Administration of--
United States--Juvenile literature. I. Title.
  HV8699.U5M66   2015
  364.660973--dc23
                                                                           2014020643

Contents

Foreword

In 2008, as the US economy and economies worldwide were falling into the worst recession since the Great Depression, most Americans had difficulty comprehending the complexity, magnitude, and scope of what was happening. As is often the case with a complex, controversial issue such as this historic global economic recession, looking at the problem as a whole can be overwhelming and often does not lead to understanding. One way to better comprehend such a large issue or event is to break it into smaller parts. The intricacies of global economic recession may be difficult to understand, but one can gain insight by instead beginning with an individual contributing factor, such as the real estate market. When examined through a narrower lens, complex issues become clearer and easier to evaluate.

This is the idea behind ReferencePoint Press's *In Controversy* series. The series examines the complex, controversial issues of the day by breaking them into smaller pieces. Rather than looking at the stem cell research debate as a whole, a title would examine an important aspect of the debate such as *Is Stem Cell Research Necessary?* or *Is Embryonic Stem Cell Research Ethical?* By studying the central issues of the debate individually, researchers gain a more solid and focused understanding of the topic as a whole.

Each book in the series provides a clear, insightful discussion of the issues, integrating facts and a variety of contrasting opinions for a solid, balanced perspective. Personal accounts and direct quotes from academic and professional experts, advocacy groups, politicians, and others enhance the narrative. Sidebars add depth to the discussion by expanding on important ideas and events. For quick reference, a list of key facts concludes every chapter. Source notes, an annotated organizations list, bibliography, and index provide student researchers with additional tools for papers and class discussion.

The *In Controversy* series also challenges students to think critically about issues, to improve their problem-solving skills, and to sharpen their ability to form educated opinions. As President Barack Obama stated in a March 2009 speech, success in the twenty-first century will not be measurable merely by students' ability to "fill in a bubble on a test but whether they possess 21st century skills like problem-solving and critical thinking and entrepreneurship and creativity." Those who possess these skills will have a strong foundation for whatever lies ahead.

No one can know for certain what sort of world awaits today's students. What we can assume, however, is that those who are inquisitive about a wide range of issues; open-minded to divergent views; aware of bias and opinion; and able to reason, reflect, and reconsider will be best prepared for the future. As the international development organization Oxfam notes, "Today's young people will grow up to be the citizens of the future: but what that future holds for them is uncertain. We can be quite confident, however, that they will be faced with decisions about a wide range of issues on which people have differing, contradictory views. If they are to develop as global citizens all young people should have the opportunity to engage with these controversial issues."

In Controversy helps today's students better prepare for tomorrow. An understanding of the complex issues that drive our world and the ability to think critically about them are essential components of contributing, competing, and succeeding in the twenty-first century.

Justice or Tragedy?

On September 21, 2011, protesters gathered outside a Georgia state prison. Inside, inmate Troy Davis was scheduled to die by lethal injection for the 1989 murder of off-duty police officer Mark MacPhail. Davis maintained he did not shoot MacPhail and witnesses had made a mistake.

In 1989 MacPhail was working a second job as a security guard when he rushed to help a homeless man who was being beaten up by a group of men that included Davis. Prosecutors alleged that when MacPhail attempted to intervene, Davis shot him to death in the parking lot. Although the gun used in the shooting was not found, prosecutors said the shell casings found at the scene were linked to an earlier shooting tied to Davis. At the time, several witnesses identified Davis as the shooter. In 1991 Davis was convicted of MacPhail's murder and sentenced to death.

In the two decades between his conviction and execution, Davis steadfastly maintained his innocence. At his trial, Davis's conviction was largely based on eyewitness testimony. Yet after his trial, seven of the nine eyewitnesses who identified Davis as the shooter recanted or contradicted their testimony. Some of them claimed that police had pressured them into making their original statements. One of those witnesses, Jeffrey Sapp, said, "I got tired of them harassing me. . . . I told them that Troy told me he did it, but it wasn't true. . . . I didn't want to have any more problems with the cops, so I testified against Troy."[1]

Davis's legal team argued in dozens of hearings before state and federal appellate courts that the lack of physical evidence and the change in eyewitness testimony should be enough reason to grant Davis a new trial. State and federal courts repeatedly ruled against Davis's requests for a new trial. In a hearing ordered by the US Supreme Court in 2010, Davis was allowed the opportunity to present evidence of his innocence in his petition for a new trial. The judge, however, ruled that although Davis had raised some doubts about his conviction, he had not provided the court with compelling evidence of his innocence. The judge denied Davis's request for a new trial.

As the September 2011 execution date drew near, hundreds of thousands of people signed petitions to spare Davis's life. People around the world called for clemency for Davis. Bob Barr, a four-term congressman from Georgia and death penalty supporter, says in an editorial he wrote on the case, "Imposing an irreversible sentence of death on the skimpiest of evidence will not serve the interest of justice."[2] A group of former death row wardens wrote to Georgia authorities asking them to halt the execution because of doubts over Davis's guilt. Davis himself offered to submit to a lie detector test, but prison officials declined. The day before his execution the Georgia Board of Pardons and Paroles rejected Davis's plea for clemency.

While many people worked to stop the execution, not everyone believed in Davis's innocence. Over the years MacPhail's family members remained convinced that Davis was guilty of murder. They fought his attempts to obtain clemency. After countless hearings and postponements, MacPhail's widow Joan, son, daughter, and mother still believed in the justice of Davis's execution for the murder of their loved one. "We have lived this for 22 years. We know what the truth is and for someone to ludicrously say he [Davis] is a victim? We are the victims. Look at us. We have put up with this stuff for 22 years and it's time for justice today,"[3] said Joan MacPhail.

Believing in his innocence, Davis's supporters staged last-minute vigils to protest his execution. Some urged prison workers to stay home. Others posted a judge's phone number online in the

> "Imposing an irreversible sentence of death on the skimpiest of evidence will not serve the interest of justice."[2]
>
> — Bob Barr, a four-term congressman from Georgia and death penalty supporter.

hope others would call and convince him to stop the execution. Several high-profile individuals, including former US president Jimmy Carter and Pope Benedict XVI, publicly called for Davis's execution to be put on hold because of the doubt over his guilt.

Despite efforts to stop the execution, the US Supreme Court denied a late request for a stay of execution. Davis entered the death chamber shortly before 11 p.m. In his final moments he once again asserted his innocence. He spoke to the MacPhail family members present, saying, "I did not personally kill your son, father, brother. All I can ask is that you look deeper into this case so you really can finally see the truth."[4] At 11:08 p.m. Davis was declared dead.

Flawed System

While MacPhail's family believes Davis's execution served justice for a crime he committed, others believe the case highlights flaws in the country's justice system. In the United States criminal defendants are considered innocent until proven guilty beyond a reasonable doubt. In Davis's case reasonable doubt appeared to exist because critical witnesses changed their testimony. Even so, the US justice system did not reconsider Davis's case or his death sentence. "Troy Davis has become an incredible symbol of everything that is broken, everything that is wrong"[5] with capital punishment in the United States, says Larry Cox, executive director of Amnesty International's US branch.

After Davis's execution, Jason Ewart, one of his lawyers, said he hoped Davis's case would lead to reforms in the country's death penalty system. "This case struck a chord in the world, and as a result the legacy of Troy Davis doesn't die tonight," he says. "Our sadness, the sadness of his friends and his family, is tempered by the hope that Troy's death will lead to fundamental legal reforms so we will never again witness, with inevitable regret, the execution of an innocent man as we did here tonight."[6]

Ongoing Debate

Public support for the death penalty (also known as capital punishment) has risen and fallen over the years, but the controversy remains intense. Supporters strongly believe the death penalty has value for deterring crime and provides just retribution for the most heinous crimes in society. On the other side, death penalty opponents argue it does not prevent crime and is applied unjustly. In addition, they point out that many nations around the world have abolished the death penalty and urge the United States to do the same.

The controversy over the death penalty has also focused on methods of execution. The widespread adoption of lethal injection for executions nationwide has sparked debate over what constitutes cruel and unusual punishment for death row inmates.

In the death penalty controversy, both supporters and opponents of the death penalty strongly feel they are justified in their beliefs. As a result, the debate over the death penalty continues to be as intense today as it has in the past.

Facts

- More than an estimated fifteen thousand Americans have been executed since the inception of the death penalty in colonial times, according to the ACLU.

- Capital punishment is legal in thirty-two US states.

- Japan is the only industrialized democracy besides the United States that has the death penalty.

What Are the Origins of the Death Penalty Controversy?

The death penalty has been used as a punishment throughout the world for many centuries. Murder was the most common crime punishable by death, as many societies believed that one who takes another's life should be required to give up his or her own life as punishment. At various times and places other crimes were also punishable by death. As far back as the eighteenth century BCE, the people of Babylon were subject to written rules that specified the punishment for certain crimes. The Code of Hammurabi, named for Babylon's king, listed at least twenty-five crimes punishable by death, including the theft of temple or palace property.

In many cases, the same punishment was not ordered for similar crimes. Instead, the punishment depended on the social status of the accused and the accuser. For example, in ancient Babylon, if a member of the upper class blinded a commoner or broke a commoner's bone, the upper-class individual would be required to pay one pound of silver as a punishment. In contrast, if a commoner hit a member of the upper class, the commoner could be flogged in public with sixty lashes of an ox-whip.

Early forms of the death penalty were designed to be slow and painful. In some societies those sentenced to death were stoned, crucified, burned at the stake, or drowned. By the eighteenth and nineteenth centuries CE, many societies decided these methods were cruel and unusual forms of punishment. They implemented faster and less painful methods of execution, including public hanging and beheading. While these methods were still violent, they were thought to be more compassionate.

The Death Penalty in America

When early colonists from Great Britain arrived in America, they brought the practice of the death penalty with them. Heavily influenced by British laws and customs, the colonies adopted English laws that included over two hundred crimes punishable by death. In 1608 the Jamestown colony of Virginia recorded the first execution in the colonies when Captain George Kendall was put to death for being a spy for Britain's greatest enemy, Spain.

Death penalty laws varied from colony to colony. In many colonies murder was the crime most commonly punishable by death. Other crimes such as arson, rape, robbery, and counterfeiting could also result in a death sentence. In the Virginia colony crimes such as stealing grapes, killing chickens, and trading with Indians could be punished by death. The New York colony could order death sentences for offenses such as striking one's mother or father or denying the true God.

Early Opposition

Around the time of the American Revolution some prominent Americans openly questioned the use of the death penalty for a wide variety of offenses. Some believed that it should only be used for the most heinous crimes, such as murder and treason. Thomas Jefferson was among those who held this belief. He introduced a bill in Virginia in 1778 to revise the colony's death penalty laws to punish only the crimes of murder and treason with death. After much debate the bill was defeated by one vote.

The death penalty was viewed in many places as a deterrent to crime, but not everyone believed that it had this effect. Benjamin

Rush, signer of the Declaration of Independence and founder of the Pennsylvania Prison Society, was one of the first Americans to organize an effort to abolish the death penalty. In 1792 Rush published a pamphlet that urged the United States to eliminate the death penalty. Rush argued that life in prison was a more effective deterrent to crime than death. Rush also argued that the death penalty did not deter crime because juries were unwilling to convict and sentence a defendant to death if they believed the punishment was too harsh for the crime.

Other prominent Americans, such as Benjamin Franklin and Philadelphia attorney general William Bradford, supported Rush's views. Like Rush, Bradford believed that the death penalty did not deter crime. Bradford cited the crime of horse stealing as an example, which in Virginia was punishable by death. Even though horse stealing was the most common crime in Virginia at the time, accused horse thieves were seldom convicted or punished. Many Virginia juries felt that the punishment of death was too severe for the crime, and this, Bradford argued, made them less likely to convict.

Subjects consult with the eighteenth-century BCE Babylonian ruler, King Hammurabi. Many historians believe that the famous law code he established was one of the first that allowed for the death penalty.

Reforms

As Rush's views gained popularity, petitions to abolish the death penalty were introduced in several state legislatures. In 1794 Pennsylvania abolished the death penalty for all crimes except murder in the first degree. It was the first time murder had been classified into degrees. A murder was deemed to be first degree if it was deliberate and planned or committed in conjunction with a felony crime such as rape or arson. Separating the crimes by degrees allowed the state to reserve the death penalty for more heinous murders.

In addition, there was a growing idea that criminals could be reformed in the late eighteenth century. This led to calls for prison sentences instead of death sentences, even in murder cases. To house the prisoners, states began to construct state prisons. In 1796 New York authorized the building of the state's first penitentiary and reduced the number of crimes punishable by death to murder and treason. Several other states followed New York's lead, building state prisons and reducing the number of crimes punishable by death. In 1846 Michigan became the first state to eliminate the death penalty for all crimes except treason and replaced the death penalty with life in prison.

In some states death penalty reforms were not applied equally to all people. Although southern states such as Kentucky and Virginia reduced the number of crimes eligible for the death penalty, these reforms did not apply to slaves. In Virginia in 1856 a black slave could be put to death for any of sixty-six different crimes. A free white person, on the other hand, could only be put to death if convicted of murder.

Mandatory Versus Discretionary Statutes

Before 1837 the death penalty for certain crimes was mandatory in all states. A person convicted of a crime that was punishable by death automatically received a death sentence. In 1837 Tennessee became the first state to pass a discretionary death penalty statute for murder. Under the new law juries could decide punishment on a case-by-case basis even for crimes that were eligible for the death penalty. Several other southern states also enacted discretionary

Intellectual Disability: *Atkins v. Virginia*

In 2002 the Supreme Court issued a landmark ruling that banned the execution of defendants with intellectual disability (previously called mental retardation). Intellectual disability is defined as significant limitations in both intellectual functioning and adaptive behavior, which affects social and life skills. Intellectual disability occurs before the age of eighteen. Mental health experts say that people with intellectual disabilities are often suggestible, and their willingness to please can cause them to confess to crimes they did not commit.

In *Atkins v. Virginia* the court ruled that the execution of defendants with intellectual disability was unconstitutional. The court determined it was a violation of the Eighth Amendment's ban on cruel and unusual punishment to execute inmates with intellectual disability. Prior to *Atkins v. Virginia*, eighteen states and the federal government did not permit the execution of those with intellectual disability.

death penalty laws. According to Robert Bohm, a criminal justice professor at the University of Central Florida, the move to discretionary statutes allowed all-white southern juries to consider race when deciding if death was the appropriate penalty. A white jury could spare the life of a defendant who had killed a black slave, but sentence to death a defendant who had killed a white man.

In some cases, the change to discretionary statutes was made to prevent juries from refusing to convict a defendant in a death penalty case. Some juries believed that mandatory death sentencing was not moral or fair. When faced with a death penalty case, they sometimes refused to convict the defendant so that he or she would not be executed. With discretionary death statutes, a jury could convict a defendant and then choose a punishment of life in prison or death. By the end of the nineteenth century more than twenty states around the country had enacted discretionary death penalty statutes. By 1963 mandatory death penalty statutes were removed from all but a handful of states across the country.

Calls to Abolish the Death Penalty

Support for the death penalty declined in many western nations after World War II. The horrors of the Holocaust, in which 6 million Jews were murdered by Germany's Nazi regime, led in 1948 to the United Nations General Assembly's adoption of the Universal Declaration of Human Rights. People in many countries interpreted this declaration as a statement of the world's opposition to the use of the death penalty. Some countries responded by abolishing the death penalty; others revised their laws to limit its use.

In the United States debate over the death penalty increased. Studies from England and Canada that were critical of the death penalty were widely read in the United States. Criminals on death row recounted their stories in books and film. In 1954 convicted kidnapper Caryl Chessman published *Cell 2455 Death Row* about his experience on death row. The book became a best seller and widely publicized Chessman's experience. Chessman spent more than eleven years on death row and received numerous stays of execution. He was executed in 1960 despite consistently proclaiming his innocence right up to the end. Chessman's story rallied many death penalty opponents to increase pressure on lawmakers to end the death penalty.

Constitutional Challenges

Trying to end the death penalty on a state-by-state basis was difficult and slow, so opponents sought to force the issue by turning to the courts. A flurry of appeals was filed in the court system in the 1960s on behalf of death row inmates who were seeking to overturn their death sentences. The appeals challenged the constitutionality of the death penalty, in most cases specifically citing the Eighth and Fourteenth Amendments.

In making their argument, death row inmates and their lawyers cited a 1958 Supreme Court decision in a case that did not involve the death penalty. In that case, known as *Trop v. Dulles*, the court wrote that the Eighth Amendment contained an "evolving standard of decency that marked the progress of a maturing society."[7] Death penalty opponents claimed that this same logic applied to state executions, saying that the United States had reached a point where its current standard of decency no longer tolerated the death penalty. Under this standard, legal teams argued, the death penalty was a form of cruel and unusual punishment—a violation of the Eighth Amendment. This amendment states, "Excessive bail shall not be required, nor excessive fines imposed, nor cruel and unusual punishments inflicted."[8] While courts around the country considered the legal issues, an unofficial moratorium on executions went into effect in July 1967 as states awaited a ruling from the Supreme Court.

The Issue Reaches the Supreme Court

The case that finally reached the Supreme Court was *Furman v. Georgia*. This 1972 case challenged the constitutionality of the death penalty under the Eighth Amendment's ban on cruel and unusual punishment. The case consolidated appeals from three men sentenced to death in Georgia and Texas. The lead case featured William Henry Furman, a twenty-six-year-old African American from Georgia. Furman had been convicted in 1968 of murder during a home break-in and robbery. Each of the other two cases, one from Georgia in 1968 and one from Texas in 1967, also involved an African American man. Each man had been convicted of sexual assault and sentenced to die.

Furman's lawyers argued the death penalty was cruel and unusual punishment according to the country's current standards of decency and therefore violated the Eighth Amendment. They contended that justice could be served with life imprisonment. The lawyers also argued that poor people and minorities received the death penalty at a vastly disproportionate rate compared to white defendants accused of similar crimes. This inequity, they argued, violated the Fourteenth Amendment's guarantee of equal protection for all people under the law.

"Excessive bail shall not be required, nor excessive fines imposed, nor cruel and unusual punishments inflicted."[8]

— Eighth Amendment, US Constitution.

Lawyers for the state of Georgia countered that the death penalty could not be considered "cruel and unusual punishment." Previous court rulings, they argued, suggested that this phrase refers to torture and barbarism and that the death penalty does not rise to the level of either. Dorothy Beasley, one of Georgia's lawyers, argued before the Supreme Court saying, "In recognizing what cruel and unusual punishment means and the cases that come out of the State Courts now, the Lower Federal Court and of this Court indicate that it means barbarous or uncivilized or torturous and that type of thing and certainly the penalty of death per se does not come within that prohibition or that understanding."[9] Georgia's lawyers also argued that the death penalty was a force for deterring crime and for satisfying public outrage over the most heinous crimes.

A Ruling in *Furman v. Georgia*

On June 29, 1972, the Supreme Court handed down its decision and overturned Furman's death sentence. The court ruled that Georgia's death penalty statute gave the jury complete sentencing discretion without sufficient guidance, a situation that could lead jurors to come up with an arbitrary sentence. As a result, the court ruled, the state's death penalty law could be considered cruel and unusual punishment and unconstitutional under the Eighth Amendment. The court's ruling also disallowed the death penalty in the companion rape cases in Georgia and Texas. It states, "The Court holds that the imposition and carrying out of the death penalty in these cases constitute cruel and unusual punishment in violation of the Eighth and Fourteenth Amendments."[10] The ruling did not find the death penalty itself to be unconstitutional. It focused instead on how the states were applying death penalty laws.

The Supreme Court ruling was not unanimous; the justices split 5–4 in their decision. The five justices who agreed the death penalty was unconstitutional cited various reasons. Justices William J. Brennan Jr.

"Cruel and unusual punishment means . . . barbarous or uncivilized or torturous and that type of thing and certainly the penalty of death per se does not come within that prohibition or that understanding."[9]

— Dorothy Beasley, lawyer for the state of Georgia in *Furman v. Georgia.*

and Thurgood Marshall reasoned the death penalty violated the Eighth Amendment regardless of crime or circumstances. Justice William O. Douglas said it was unconstitutional because it was applied in a discriminatory manner. He wrote, "We deal with a system of law and of justice that leaves to the uncontrolled discretion of judges or juries the determination whether defendants committing these crimes should die or be imprisoned. Under these laws no standards govern the selection of the penalty. People live or die, dependent on the whim of one man or of 12."[11] Justice Marshall also noted that the arbitrary application of the death penalty was unconstitutional, writing: "It also is evident that the burden of capital punishment falls upon the poor, the

During World War II, the Nazis established death camps where Jews, homosexuals, and others deemed undesirable were executed. Victims such as those pictured at the infamous Dachau concentration camp sparked worldwide opposition to the death penalty.

ignorant, and the underprivileged members of society. It is the poor, and the members of minority groups who are least able to voice their complaints against capital punishment. Their impotence leaves them victims of a sanction that the wealthier, better-represented, just-as-guilty person can escape."[12]

Chief Justice Warren E. Burger and justices Harry Blackmun, Lewis F. Powell Jr., and William Rehnquist dissented from the majority opinion, stating that the death penalty had long been considered an appropriate punishment for serious crimes in the United States. In his dissent Burger wrote that he could not agree with characterizations of the death penalty as it was practiced in the United States as cruel and unusual: "Punishments are cruel when they involve torture or a lingering death; but the punishment of death is not cruel within the meaning of that word as used in the Constitution. It implies there something inhuman and barbarous, something more than the mere extinguishment of life."[13]

Mandatory Sentences

Within four years of the *Furman* decision, thirty-five states had rewritten and implemented new death penalty statutes, many of which were again challenged in court. Some of the new statutes called for mandatory sentencing, which required an automatic death sentence if a defendant was found guilty of first-degree murder. States such as North Carolina argued that mandatory sentencing eliminated the possibility of arbitrary or discriminatory jury decisions, thus eliminating the problem cited in the *Furman* case. But in 1976 the Supreme Court ruled in a North Carolina case that mandatory sentencing was also unconstitutional. In the ruling, Justice Potter Stewart explained that mandatory sentencing reduces the possibility of juries treating similar cases in different ways. However, he added, it also requires juries to ignore the specific circumstances of a given case in deciding the sentence—a situation that could also lead to an arbitrary or unreasonable sentence.

Guided Discretion

Not all states followed the mandatory sentencing route. After the *Furman* decision, some sought to make their laws constitutional by adopting guided discretion statutes. These statutes require juries in death penalty cases to follow statewide guidelines for determining sentences in first-degree murder cases. Under these laws, during the sentencing phase juries could consider a defendant's background and character and the circumstances of the crime. Opponents of the death penalty also challenged guided discretion statutes, arguing that they too represented cruel and unusual punishment.

The Supreme Court considered the constitutionality of these laws in a 1976 case, *Gregg v. Georgia*. The defendant in the case, Troy Gregg, had been convicted of murder and armed robbery in 1974 and sentenced to death in Georgia. He appealed his sentence, specifically citing how the state had applied its guided discretion statutes to his case.

After the *Furman* decision Georgia, like many states, had rewritten its death penalty statute. The state established a bifurcated trial process, which separated the guilt and sentencing phases so that a defendant's guilt or innocence was determined in one trial, and the sentence was decided in a second trial. The state also developed a list of aggravating circumstances. A jury had to find beyond a reasonable doubt that an aggravating circumstance applied to the crime before it could sentence the defendant to death. The defendant was also allowed to present to the jury mitigating circumstances that might convince them to recommend a sentence other than death. Mitigating circumstances included the age of the defendant, his or her cooperation with police, and emotional state at the time of the crime. If the jury sentenced a defendant to death, the Georgia Supreme Court automatically reviewed the decision.

In Gregg's case, a jury had found him guilty in the first phase of the trial. In the sentencing trial that followed, the jury found beyond a reasonable doubt that Gregg had committed the murders during the commission of another capital crime and for the pur-

"The punishment of death is not cruel within the meaning of that word as used in the Constitution. It implies there something inhuman and barbarous, something more than the mere extinguishment of life."[13]

— Warren E. Burger, US Supreme Court justice.

Death Sentences and Juveniles

Many people believe that juveniles who commit crimes are not as responsible for their actions as adults are. In addition, many believe juvenile offenders can be rehabilitated into productive adults. Therefore, many people strongly oppose the execution of juvenile inmates.

For many years some states had no minimum age for executions. For example, in 1946 two fourteen-year-olds convicted of murder were executed in Mississippi. In 1988 the Supreme Court ruled in *Thompson v. Oklahoma* that executing an inmate who had committed a crime at age fifteen or younger was cruel and unusual punishment and banned by the Eighth Amendment. In 1989 the Supreme Court ruled that execution of inmates who had committed crimes at ages sixteen or seventeen was not prohibited.

In 2005 the Supreme Court expanded its ban on the death penalty in *Roper v. Simmons* and ruled that the death penalty for inmates who had committed their crimes when they were under eighteen years of age was a form of cruel and unusual punishment and therefore unconstitutional.

pose of taking a victim's property. Both of these were considered aggravating factors that allowed them to sentence him to death.

When the case came before the Supreme Court, the justices upheld Gregg's sentence. They found that Georgia's system of applying the death penalty was judicious and careful and upheld the constitutionality of the death penalty. The court reasoned that the death sentence was not arbitrary because the new statutes restricted and guided the prosecutors, judges, and juries. The court stated,

The basic concern of Furman centered on those defendants who were being condemned to death capriciously and arbitrarily. Under the procedures before the Court in that case, sentencing authorities were not directed to give attention to the nature or circumstances of the crime committed or to the character or record of the defendant. Left unguided, juries imposed the death sentence in a way that could only be called freakish. The new Georgia sentencing procedures, by contrast, focus the jury's attention on the particularized nature of the crime and the particularized characteristics of the individual defendant. While the jury is permitted to consider any aggravating or mitigating circumstances, it must find and identify at least one statutory aggravating factor before it may impose a penalty of death. In this way, the jury's discretion is channeled.[14]

In addition, the court approved other procedural changes in the *Gregg* decision. These included the practice of automatic appellate review of all convictions and sentences and a proportionality review. The latter involved a comparison between the current case and other cases in the state to ensure that the death penalty was applied fairly. The following year, in 1977, the ten-year moratorium on executions ended in the United States.

The Debate Today

Public support for the death penalty has declined in recent years. According to a 2013 Gallup poll, 60 percent of Americans say they favor the death penalty for convicted murderers. This is the lowest level of support measured by Gallup since 1972, when 57 percent of Americans said they favored the death penalty. Yet the death penalty remains law in many states. As of mid-2014, thirty-two states along with the federal government and the US military had the death penalty.

Advances in science, particularly DNA testing, have played an increasing role in establishing a defendant's guilt or innocence. Several states have placed moratoriums on the death penalty after death row inmates were proved innocent of the crimes for which they were convicted. Since 2007 six states have repealed their death penalty laws entirely. However, the debate over the death penalty continues.

Facts

- Between 1976, when the US Supreme Court ended a nationwide moratorium on the death penalty, and April 2014, a total of 1,378 people were executed in the United States, according to the Death Penalty Information Center (DPIC).

- Since 1976 twenty-two defendants were executed for crimes committed as juveniles, reports the DPIC.

- Over two-thirds of countries around the world have abolished the death penalty.

- Nationwide, executions and death sentences have dropped by half since 2000.

- In 2010 in the United States, 1 out of every 326 murders ended in a death sentence, reports the DPIC.

- The United States ranked fifth worldwide for number of executions in 2012, behind China, Iran, Iraq, and Saudi Arabia.

CHAPTER TWO

Is the Death Penalty Just Retribution for the Worst Crimes?

I n January 2014 US attorney general Eric Holder announced federal prosecutors would seek the death penalty in the trial of Dzhokhar Tsarnaev, the defendant accused of setting off two bombs at the 2013 Boston Marathon. The bomb explosions killed three people and wounded more than 260 others. Prosecutors allege that Tsarnaev committed this act with his older brother Tamerlan Tsarnaev, who was killed in a shootout with police days after the bombing. "After consideration of the relevant facts, the applicable regulations and the submissions made by the defendant's counsel, I have determined that the United States will seek the death penalty in this matter," Holder says in a statement. "The nature of the conduct at issue and the resultant harm compel this decision."[15] Over half of the thirty federal charges against Tsarnaev carry a possible death sentence, including using weapons of mass destruction.

After Holder's announcement federal prosecutors filed a notice with the court listing factors they believe justify the death penalty

Mitigating and Aggravating Factors

During the penalty phase of a murder trial the jury considers the appropriate punishment for the crime. When deciding if the defendant should live or die, the jury often considers mitigating and aggravating factors. Mitigating factors are evidence presented about the defendant's character or the circumstances of the crime that would cause a juror to vote for a lesser sentence. An example of a mitigating factor is evidence of the defendant's extreme mental or emotional distress at the time of the crime. Aggravating factors are evidence presented regarding the defendant's character or the circumstances of the crime that would cause a juror to vote for a harsher sentence. An example of an aggravating factor would be evidence that the crime was planned in advance or performed for money. Every state has its own laws that instruct jurors how to consider aggravating and mitigating factors during a sentencing trial.

in Tsarnaev's case. They cited the fact that the attack killed multiple people and required substantial planning and premeditation, among other factors. Federal officials also weighed the opinions of the victims when deciding whether to pursue the death penalty. They asked survivors to complete a questionnaire to determine their views on the death penalty. One survivor, Marc Fucarile, says he believes Tsarnaev deserves to die for his role in the bombings. "I prefer the death penalty, because I prefer that people know that if you terrorize our country, you're going to be put to death. And I strongly believe that's how it should be,"[16] says Fucarile, who lost a leg in the bombing.

Given the heinous nature and enormity of the attack, legal analysts are not surprised that federal prosecutors will seek the death penalty for Tsarnaev if he is found guilty at trial. "This is a case, that, if you believe in the death penalty, seems to cry out for the death penalty, even though the defendant is only 19 years old, and potentially the junior partner to his late brother,"[17] says CNN senior legal analyst Jeffrey Toobin.

Public opinion is mixed over the appropriate punishment if Tsarnaev is found guilty. For some, execution is a just penalty for a heinous crime. "A lot of people were hurt, and a lot of families were affected," says Boston resident Alicia Jno-Baptiste, who supports the death penalty for Tsarnaev if convicted. "They intended to kill thousands of people." Life without parole is insufficient, she says, because "you still get to live. You're still alive. You can still be happy. The people they were trying to kill, they won't be able to do that stuff. He knows what he intended to do, and I think he could live with that in jail and be pretty OK."[18]

Yet others believe execution may not be the right answer. In a September 2013 poll of Boston residents conducted by the *Boston Globe*, 57 percent of respondents supported a sentence of life without parole if Tsarnaev is convicted of the marathon attack. Only 33 percent of respondents said they favored the death penalty in the case. "Whatever he's alleged to have done, presumably he can pay for it with his life. Putting this boy to death doesn't make any sense to me,"[19] says Amato DeLuca, a lawyer for Tamerlan Tsarnaev's widow.

Crimes Eligible for the Death Penalty

In the United States the death penalty is used almost exclusively in cases where defendants are convicted of murder or conspiracy to commit murder. Not every murder is eligible for the death penalty. State by state, the factors that allow a defendant convicted of murder to be sentenced to death vary. In many states—among them Alabama, Pennsylvania, and Arkansas—a prosecutor can seek the death penalty only when there are aggravating circumstances in connection with the murder. In Alabama an aggravating circumstance exists if the crime was committed as one of a series of intentional killings; in Pennsylvania, an aggravating circumstance exists if the victim was under twelve years of age. Other aggravating circumstances include prior felony convictions, kidnapping or raping the murder victim, and premeditation.

Boston Marathon participants run toward the finish line shortly after a bomb explodes, taking the lives of three people. Despite the heinous nature of the crime, only a minority of Boston residents favor the death penalty for bombing suspect, Dzhokhar Tsarnaev.

Some state and federal statutes include other crimes that are eligible for the death penalty. These crimes include treason, aggravated kidnapping, espionage, aircraft hijacking, and large-scale drug trafficking. Since the death penalty was reinstated in 1976, no one has been executed for a non-murder offense.

In the early history of the United States, the crime of rape (now commonly known as sexual assault) was punishable by death in some states. In recent decades, however, the courts have banned the death penalty in rape cases. In 1977 the US Supreme Court ruled in *Coker v. Georgia* that the death penalty was an excessive punishment for the rape of an adult, ruling it was unconstitutional under the Eighth Amendment. Some states still allowed prosecutors to seek the death penalty in cases that involved the rape of a child. In 2008 the Supreme Court ruled in *Kennedy v. Louisiana* that the death penalty was not appropriate for crimes against an individual that did not involve the death of the victim, even in cases involving the rape of child.

Retribution for Heinous Crimes

Retribution is one of the oldest justifications for the death penalty, dating back to the earliest systems of justice. Under the idea of retribution, a criminal should be punished in proportion to the crime he or she committed. In this view, a just punishment for a heinous murder is the execution of the murderer.

Ohio state representative Jim Buchy is among those who believe that the death penalty is justified for those who commit brutal murders. In 1989 Buchy was the state representative of Preble County, Ohio, where the murder of Joy Stewart occurred. At the time of her death, Stewart was a twenty-two-year-old newlywed and eight months pregnant. Stewart was brutally raped and stabbed; the attack killed both her and her fetus. Stewart's killer was executed in 2014. "I remember the surprise and outrage of the residents and families upon learning about the heinous murder, and I know I share the opinion of many throughout the area and all across Ohio that justice was served when the killer was put to death."[20]

Buchy believes the death penalty allows society to clearly state that human life is valuable and that those who destroy a human life must pay for their actions in equal measure. "I simply believe that life is a precious thing, and therefore taking the life of someone else should be met with equal retribution. If the murderer did not think his victims deserved to live, then how can he be so sure he was either?"[21]

George Brauchler, district attorney for Colorado's Eighteenth Judicial District, also views the death penalty as just punishment for the worst murders. In 2013 Colorado lawmakers debated whether to repeal that state's death penalty statute. Brauchler argued for retaining the state's death penalty law because it allows prosecutors to differentiate between murder offenses and to consider aggravating factors. He comments in the *Denver Post*,

> It is common sense that a criminal's sentence potentially may be enhanced based on the heinous nature of their act,

"I remember the surprise and outrage of the residents and families upon learning about the heinous murder, and I know I share the opinion of many throughout the area and all across Ohio that justice was served when the killer was put to death."[20]

— Jim Buchy, Ohio state representative.

the number of victims, the age and type of victim, and whether the offender is a repeat offender. A third DUI [driving under the influence of alcohol conviction] is punished more harshly than a first. A crime spree involving numerous burglaries leads to a longer sentence than a single break-in. Assaulting a child is more aggravated than the same assault on an adult. A convicted felon who commits a new crime is incarcerated longer than a first-time offender. One size does not fit all. This is justice.

If Colorado were to repeal the death penalty, first-degree murder would become the only crime for which no distinction is made for the number of murders committed, the aggravated nature of the murder, whether the victim is a child or an at-risk adult, or even whether a previously convicted murderer kills yet again. Repealing the death penalty would result in acts similar to those in Newtown, Conn., or the acts of [Oklahoma City federal building bomber] Tim McVeigh being punished no differently than a single murder of one gang member by another. Each murder after the first would be a freebie. This is not justice.[22]

Prevents Vigilante Justice

Over time the death penalty has also been viewed as a way to control and prevent vigilante actions. In the late nineteenth and early twentieth centuries acts of vigilante justice were common in parts of the United States, especially when people believed the legal system could not or would not carry out justice. When Colorado abolished the death penalty in 1897, angry mobs turned to lynching. After several lynchings took place, concerned citizens called for the death penalty to be reinstated. This, they hoped, would stop people from taking justice into their own hands and provide just punishment for terrible crimes.

In 1900 in Limon, Colorado, a sixteen-year-old black youth, John Preston Porter Jr., was accused of sexually assaulting and

Deterrence

For some the death penalty is necessary because it deters crime. If criminals know that they can be put to death for a crime, they may think twice before committing it. Someone who robs a store may spare the life of the cashier. A murderer who faces significant jail time may decide not to commit additional murders if it spares his or her life.

"Without the potential for a death sentence, there is no incentive for a murderer on the run not to kill again in order to avoid being caught—even if that murder is of a police officer or 10 police officers," says George Brauchler, district attorney for Colorado's Eighteenth Judicial District. "There would be no incentive for a defendant awaiting his murder trial not to try to kill a key witness, the judge, or perhaps the prosecutor on his case. There would be no disincentive for inmates serving life sentences from killing each other or prison guards, because the result of such evil would be . . . the loss of cable TV? Less Jell-o at dinner? No more shooting hoops outside? This is not justice, and it makes our community less safe."

George Brauchler, "Death Penalty Is a Tool of Justice," *Denver Post*, March 31, 2013. www.denverpost.com.

murdering a young white girl. Even before trial, local newspapers pronounced Porter guilty. An editorial in the *Denver Post* stated,

> The laws of Colorado, since the repeal of the law legalizing hanging, provide no adequate punishment for such inhuman brutes as those who commit outrageous crimes like that at Limon. Indeed, with capital punishment abolished there is in such cases a direct invitation to the outraged people to take the law into their own hands and visit upon the head of the brutal murderer such condign [deserved] punishment as cannot fail to shock the whole community. . . . A

few more object lessons will doubtless convince the people of the state that capital punishment should be restored to the statute books. While it may be true that ordinary life or long term imprisonment may be a fit punishment for the crime committed, there are times when nothing short of the death penalty will satisfy the demands of justice.[23]

A mob of three hundred met the train carrying Porter to Limon for his trial. They brought him to the site of the murder, tied him to a stake, set him on fire, and burned him to death. After Porter's killing, Colorado reinstated the death penalty in 1901. Nearly seventy years later, the role of the death penalty in providing just retribution through legal avenues was explained by Supreme Court justice Potter Stewart in the 1972 *Furman* case. In that case Stewart writes, "The instinct for retribution is part of the nature of man. And channeling that instinct in the administration of the criminal justice serves an important purpose in promoting the stability of a society governed by law. When people begin to believe that organized society is unwilling or unable to impose upon criminal offenders the punishment they 'deserve,' then there are sown the seeds of anarchy—of self-help, vigilante justice, and lynch law."[24]

Relief for Family and Friends

The death penalty can also be viewed as providing desperately needed finality and relief for a victim's family and friends. While the execution of a murderer cannot bring back a loved one, it can allow surviving family members to move forward with their lives and accept their loss. The death penalty's finality can bring peace of mind and a belief that justice has been done for the victim's family and friends.

For two decades Lera Shelley waited for the execution of Michael Ross, a serial killer who murdered her daughter. She says the wait was worth it when she finally witnessed Ross die in May 2005 by lethal injection at Connecticut's Osborn Correctional Institution. "When I saw Michael Ross take his last breath, I knew it was all over. No more appeals, no more 'Walking with Michael' [Ross's prison writings] on the Internet," says Shelley. In her eyes, Ross's execution brought justice for her daughter and the seven other women Ross murdered. His death gave her the finality and closure she needed to move on with her life. "It was like a big cloud that had been hanging over our head for years had finally been lifted and sunshine was coming in,"[25] says Shelley.

More Harm to Victims' Families

While many victims' family members support the death penalty, a growing number do not. For some, the death penalty process causes more pain and suffering. After a conviction the path to execution can take years, even decades. According to the Death Pen-

Originally sentenced to death by hanging in Washington State, convicted murderer, Mitchell Rupe had his sentence commuted to life imprisonment without parole when an appeals court ruled that hanging was cruel and unusual punishment. In 1997, the Supreme Court rejected efforts to reinstate Rupe's death sentence.

alty Information Center, inmates typically spend over ten years on death row. Some inmates have been on death row for over twenty years. During that time, the victim's family members endure numerous appeals and press coverage. The details of the crime are relived repeatedly. For some family members this process can be severely traumatic.

In 2012 Washington senator Debbie Regala, who lost a family member to murder in 1980, spoke along with other victims' family members at a press conference and urged the Washington legislature to repeal the state's death penalty. They asked the legislature to replace it with life in prison without parole. Regala said the death penalty is a broken system that fails to offer closure to victims' families and does not deter future crime. "Does the death penalty bring back my family member? The answer is *no*. Did existence of the death penalty prevent that crime? *Obviously not*. And would continuing the death penalty prevent future murders? Again, the facts would indicate *no*,"[26] states Regala.

The lengthy appeals process for people on death row is another reason cited by some family members for eliminating the death penalty. Karil Klingbeil, whose sister Candy was murdered in 1981 by Mitchell Rupe, says that her initial support for the death penalty has changed over time. After enduring two decades of appeals, Klingbeil now views life in prison without chance of parole as an appropriate punishment for murder—and as a way for family members to heal from the horror they have experienced. "Had Rupe received life without parole after the first trial, my family would have been spared 20 years of additional suffering. We would have been able to honor Candy's memory and begin the healing process."[27]

Kathleen Garcia is a victims' advocate and an expert in traumatic grief. She served on the New Jersey Death Penalty Study Commission, which investigated the impact of the death penalty on family members. Because of Garcia's own work with victims' families, she believes the death penalty harms victim's families and

> "Had Rupe received life without parole after the first trial, my family would have been spared 20 years of additional suffering. We would have been able to honor Candy's memory and begin the healing process."[27]
>
> — Karil Klingbeil, whose sister Candy was murdered in 1981 by Mitchell Rupe.

should be replaced by life in prison. "Make no mistake—I am a conservative, a victims' advocate and a death penalty supporter. But my real life experience has taught me that as long as the death penalty is on the books in any form, it will continue to harm survivors. For that reason alone, it must be ended," says Garcia. "I don't have any compassion for murderers and believe they deserve harsh and certain punishment. In real life, the death penalty doesn't work that way. . . . I have watched too many families go through this over the years to believe that there is any way to make the system work better. Even in those states that do carry out executions, most cases are reversed at some point. I've known people in New Jersey whose entire childhoods were lost waiting for an execution that never came. They endured multiple trials, as well as the additional trauma each one created in their fractured lives, leaving them feeling re-victimized by the very system they once trusted to give them some sense of justice."[28]

Taking a Life Is Wrong

Death penalty opponents argue that executing a defendant is not justice. They believe taking a life is wrong under any circumstances. All life is precious, even that of a murderer. "A capital punishment is always tragic news, a reason for sadness, even if it deals with a person who is guilty of grave crimes," says the Reverend Frederico Lombardi, a Vatican spokesperson. "The killing of the guilty party is not the way to reconstruct justice and reconcile society. On the contrary, there is a risk that it will feed a spirit of vendetta and sow new violence."[29]

> "The death penalty is the ultimate, irreversible denial of human rights."[30]
>
> — Amnesty International, a human rights organization.

Organizations such as Amnesty International, which works to end human rights abuses worldwide, considers government-sanctioned executions to be the ultimate violation of human rights. The organization states, "The death penalty is the ultimate, irreversible denial of human rights. It is the premeditated and cold-blooded killing of a human being by the state. It violates the right to life as proclaimed in the Universal Declaration of Human Rights, and the right to be free from cruel, inhuman, and degrading punishment."[30]

At its core, the belief that the death penalty either is or is not just retribution for the most heinous crimes in society is a moral and emotional issue. For some, killing another human, no matter the reason or circumstances, is wrong and unjust. For others, when an innocent victim is killed a life for a life is the only way justice can be served. With people on both sides of the issue holding strong beliefs, it is likely the controversy over how to achieve justice will not end anytime soon.

Facts

- In the sentencing phase of a death penalty case all jurors must vote in favor of death in order to sentence a defendant to death. If only one juror votes against the death penalty, the jury must recommend life in prison.

- A proportionality review compares a death sentence in one case with the sentences handed down for similar crimes in the state to ensure fairness.

- Timothy McVeigh was the first person executed under the reinstated federal death penalty for the 1995 bombing of the Oklahoma City federal building, which killed 167 people.

- A 2013 Gallup poll found 62 percent of Americans believe the death penalty is morally acceptable, while 31 percent consider it morally wrong.

- In 2013, 18 percent of Americans said they strongly favor the death penalty—a decline from 28 percent who said this in 2011, according to the Pew Research Center.

Is the Risk of Executing an Innocent Person Too High?

In September 2012 thirty-eight-year-old Damon Thibodeaux was released from the Louisiana State Penitentiary after spending fifteen years on death row for a murder he did not commit. That murder took place in 1996 near New Orleans, Louisiana. The victim was fourteen-year-old Crystal Champagne, Thibodeaux's step-cousin. On the afternoon of July 19, 1996, Champagne left her apartment to go to a local supermarket. She never returned. Her body was found the next day near a levee in Bridge City, Louisiana. Police interviewed several people about the murder, including Thibodeaux. After being interrogated by police for nine hours Thibodeaux confessed under pressure to raping and murdering the girl. Based on this confession Thibodeaux was convicted and sentenced to death in 1997.

A decade later Thibodeaux's legal team presented new evidence of his innocence. An investigation eventually exonerated Thibodeaux. That investigation included DNA testing, testing of forensic evidence from the crime scene, and repeat interviews with witnesses. "The probe confirmed that Thibodeaux's confession was false in every significant aspect,"[31] says the American Civil Liberties Union (ACLU).

Quality Reviews

To prevent wrongful convictions and ultimately wrongful executions, some people believe that the criminal justice system should develop quality control procedures. Many workplaces have such procedures. Food and drug makers undergo rigorous safety and quality testing of products. In hospitals, staff conferences examine why patients died and review doctor and staff actions. Airline pilots have a system to submit concerns about aircraft safety. In all of these industries quality reviews and testing identifies errors and helps prevent them from happening in the future. In the criminal justice system a quality control program would review overturned convictions, identify weaknesses in the justice system, and develop safeguards to prevent future errors, wrongful convictions, and wrongful executions.

District attorneys' offices in New York City, Dallas, and Santa Clara, California, have launched conviction-review units. The units review cases that defense lawyers bring to them and can investigate new leads. Sometimes after reviewing the evidence, these units agree to ask a judge to overturn a conviction. In 2014 Brooklyn district attorney Kenneth Thompson asked the court to overturn the murder conviction of Jonathan Fleming after determining through a case review that the Brooklyn murder occurred while Fleming was vacationing in Disney World. Fleming had served twenty-five years in prison for his wrongful conviction. These departments hope that their quality control efforts will prevent innocent people from being convicted and, in the worst cases, executed.

Denise LeBoeuf, director of the ACLU Capital Punishment Project, has represented Thibodeaux since 1998. Thibodeaux's case, she says, is an example of a flawed justice system that can too easily and too often go awry. The risk of errors—in procedures, in witness testimony, and even in the handling of evidence—is simply too great to keep death penalty laws in place. She argues they should be abolished. "It doesn't make us safer; it makes the pain of murder worse; and if we can't figure out how to have a death penalty that doesn't put innocent men on death row and innocent women on death row across the country, then we don't deserve to have it. It is a human rights violation. We need to end it now,"[32] she says.

Wrongful Convictions

Every year in the United States mistakes occur in the justice system, and people like Damon Thibodeaux go to jail for crimes they did not commit. Since 1989 more than two thousand people have been convicted and later exonerated of serious crimes, according to researchers from the University of Michigan Law School and the Center on Wrongful Convictions at Northwestern University School of Law. Some of these convictions occurred because defendants pled guilty to a crime they did not commit in order to avoid a longer prison sentence. Others were exonerated because of new evidence in their cases, including witness testimony and DNA evidence, or after investigations revealed corrupt practices by police, including the planting of evidence. When a mistake occurs in a death penalty case, an innocent person could be put to death.

The National Registry of Exonerations reported a record high of eighty-seven people who were exonerated for false convictions in 2013. Almost half of the cases involved murder convictions, while eighteen exonerations applied to rape or sexual assault cases. In October 2011 fifty-seven-year-old Michael Morton was released from prison after spending twenty-five years behind bars for a wrongful murder conviction. In August 1986 Morton's wife, Christine, was attacked and killed at their home in Williamson County, Texas. Although Morton was at work during the killing, police suspected he murdered his wife. They charged him with murder and put him on trial. "Innocent people think that if you just tell the truth then you've got noth-

"If we can't figure out how to have a death penalty that doesn't put innocent men on death row and innocent women on death row across the country, then we don't deserve to have it."[32]

— Denise LeBoeuf, director of the ACLU Capital Punishment Project.

Michael Morton (center), convicted of murdering his wife, was released from prison in October 2011 after twenty-five years when DNA evidence helped prove his innocence. His case let to a new Texas law aimed at preventing the types of errors that led to Morton's wrongful conviction.

ing to fear from the police," says Morton. "If you just stick to it that the system will work, it'll all come to light, everything will be fine." Even during the trial, Morton believed his innocence would eventually prevail. "There was no scientific evidence, there was no eyewitness, there was no murder weapon, there was no believable motive," says Morton. "I didn't see how any rational, thinking person would say that's enough for a guilty verdict."[33] Even so, the jury convicted Morton. The jury foreman, Mark Landrum, says the jurors felt strongly that they were doing the right thing and providing justice for Christine.

Morton spent the next twenty-five years in jail until a group of attorneys uncovered the truth. They presented evidence that the prosecutor in Morton's case had withheld important evidence during Morton's trial that would have supported his claims of innocence. Morton's son, who was only three years old in 1986, had seen and described his mother's attacker and told relatives that his father was not home at the time of the attack. Neighbors of the Mortons had also described a strange man with a green van near the house on the day of the murder. In addition, a bloody bandana was found near the Morton house. None of this evidence was presented during the trial. After years of legal fighting Morton's attorneys were able to have the bloody bandana tested for DNA. The crime lab discovered the bandana held Christine Morton's blood and hair. It also contained the blood of a convicted felon named Mark Norwood. Norwood has since been convicted in Christine's murder.

The increased precision of DNA testing has allowed legal teams to clear more wrongfully convicted defendants. In addition, an increased focus by police and prosecutors to look into cases in which questions had been raised has also led to exonerations. In fact, many of the exonerations reported in 2013 were initiated by law enforcement. "Police and prosecutors have become more attentive and concerned about the danger of false conviction," says registry editor Samuel Gross, a Michigan law professor. "We are working harder to identify the mistakes we made years ago, and we are catching more of them." Gross adds, "DNA has taught us a huge amount about the criminal justice system. Biological evidence has forced all of us to realize that we've made a lot of mistakes. But most exonerations involve shoe-leather, not DNA."[34]

"Police and prosecutors have become more attentive and concerned about the danger of false conviction. We are working harder to identify the mistakes we made years ago, and we are catching more of them."[34]

— Samuel Gross, a Michigan law professor.

Factors in Wrongful Convictions

To better understand and prevent wrongful convictions, the Innocence Project, an advocacy group for prisoners seeking exoneration, has worked for more than fifteen years to identify the factors that lead to wrongful conviction. According to the Innocence Project, 73 percent of the post-conviction exoneration cases they track involve witnesses who mistakenly identify a defendant. Many times these misidentifications involve cross-racial identification, as research has shown that people have more difficulty recognizing faces of a different race than their own.

Improper forensic science also contributes to wrongful convictions in 50 percent of cases later overturned. Mistakes can be made

Michael Morton Act

Legislation that helps the criminal justice system prevent wrongful conviction is an important safeguard for all cases, including death penalty cases. In 2013 Texas legislators passed a bill known as the Michael Morton Act. The act requires prosecutors to give defendants access to their files and keep records of the evidence they disclose to the defense. While federal law requires prosecutors to give the defense any evidence that supports guilt or punishment, the act goes further and requires prosecutors to disclose all police reports and witness statements, whether or not the evidence is being used to support guilt or punishment.

The act was named after defendant Michael Morton who was wrongfully convicted for the murder of his wife and sentenced to life in prison in 1987. In 2011 he was released and exonerated after DNA evidence proved that another person had committed the murder. Although Morton had not been sentenced to death, the mistakes made by the prosecution in his case could easily occur in a death penalty case. In Morton's case, the prosecutor withheld evidence from trial that could have been used to prove Morton's innocence. "This is a great day for fairness in Texas. The Michael Morton Act will reduce wrongful convictions; it is something we can all be very proud of," says Kathryn Kase, executive director of the Texas Defender Service, which represents death row inmates.

Quoted in Brandi Grissom, "Perry Signs Michael Morton Act," *Texas Tribune*, May 16, 2013. www.texastribune.org.

in several forensic tests, including hair microscopy, bite mark comparisons, firearm tool mark analysis, and shoe print comparisons. In addition, some forensic tests such as blood typing can be improperly performed, leading to incorrect results.

False confessions and incriminating statements also contribute to wrongful convictions. In homicide cases false confessions are the leading cause of wrongful convictions. In some cases suspects are coerced by police into confessing in order to avoid harsher punishments. Other times informants provide false information that leads to a wrongful conviction. In some cases the police offer informants deals, special treatment, or dropping of charges against them in return for testimony against a defendant. These incentives can sometimes cause an informant to provide incorrect and unreliable testimony at trial, which can influence a jury.

Risk of Executing the Innocent

Death penalty cases are just as susceptible to these factors as other cases. Since 1973 over 140 people have been released from death row in twenty-six states after being exonerated of the crimes for which they were convicted and sentenced, the ACLU reports. It is likely that others who await execution face this penalty for crimes they did not commit. A study released in 2014 by the Justice Department and the Death Penalty Information Center estimates that as many as one in twenty-five inmates on death rows in states across the country are innocent.

The number of exonerations in all cases, but especially in death penalty cases, is reason enough to repeal death penalty laws, opponents say. The risk of executing even one innocent person is too high. Columbia University law professor James Liebman and a team of students believe this is exactly what happened in the case of Carlos DeLuna. DeLuna was executed in Texas in 1989 for the 1983 stabbing murder of a gas station clerk in Corpus Christi. In 2012 Liebman and his team presented evidence that they believe proves Texas executed an innocent man. DeLuna claimed all along, up until his execution, that he was innocent of the crime. Liebman's research, published in the *Columbia Human Rights Law Review*, claims that poor police work, the prosecution's failure to investigate another suspect, and a weak defense contributed to DeLuna's death sentence. "I would say that across the board, there was nonchalance," says Liebman. "It looked like a common case, but we found that there was a very serious claim of innocence."[35]

Leibman says the case against DeLuna rested on eyewitness testimony. A customer at the gas station told police that he saw DeLuna putting a knife in his pocket outside the store. Another customer identified DeLuna as the man seen leaving the store after the murder. A third witness identified DeLuna as a man seen running a few blocks away from the crime scene. Because DeLuna had been arrested in the past for burglary, public drunkenness, attempted rape, and auto theft, the police believed they had found the murderer. Yet Liebman's legal team believes DeLuna was the victim of mistaken identity. They found the eyewitness statements in the trial conflicted with each other, blood evidence was not found on DeLuna, and a second suspect who looked like DeLuna was never investigated. "If a new trial was somehow able to be conducted today, a jury would acquit DeLuna," says Richard Dieter, executive director of the Death Penalty Information Center, who read a draft of Liebman's report. "We don't have a perfect case where [we] can agree that we have an innocent person who's been executed, but by weight of this investigation, I think we can say this is as close as a person is going to come."[36]

Enough doubt has surfaced in DeLuna's case, Liebman says, to support the possibility that an innocent person has been executed in the past and could be executed in the future. He believes the death penalty should be repealed across the country to prevent such a tragedy from occurring. "There are many cases out there that nobody has ever looked at and are probably at risk of innocence," says Liebman. "It's a cautionary tale about the risks we take when we have the death penalty."[37]

> "There are many cases out there that nobody has ever looked at and are probably at risk of innocence. It's a cautionary tale about the risks we take when we have the death penalty."[37]
>
> — James Liebman, Columbia University law professor.

Repeal of Death Penalty Statutes

Some states have already decided the risk of executing an innocent person is too high. States such as New Jersey, Connecticut, and Illinois either have repealed death penalty statutes or have imposed a moratorium on executions. Illinois governor George Ryan declared a moratorium on executions in his state in 2000 after several death row inmates were discovered to be innocent of the crimes for which they were convicted and sentenced. In 2011 the Illinois General Assembly banned the death penalty entirely. "No innocent person will ever be executed in the state of Illinois," says David Protess, director of the Medill Innocence Project, which works to clear the names of falsely condemned death row prisoners. "No person will ever go to death row for a crime they did not commit."[38]

Diann Rust-Tierney, executive director of the National Coalition Against the Death Penalty, supports the Illinois ban. She believes it was needed because of fault found in the state's ability to handle death penalty cases. "Illinois had to confront the issue," says Rust-Tierney. "Can we countenance a system that can't tell the difference between the innocent and the guilty?"[39]

Checks and Balances Protect the Innocent

While death penalty opponents argue that flaws in the legal system could lead to the execution of an innocent person, others say the risk of such a tragic mistake is exceedingly low. The justice system has numerous built-in checks and balances to prevent just such an occurrence. "A just system of capital punishment in our legal system requires procedures that ensure that only those deserving of the ultimate punishment are sentenced to death, and that the public have confidence in the adequacy of the criminal justice system to that task,"[40] says Jennifer Laurin, a professor at the University of Texas at Austin School of Law.

Every person sentenced to death is entitled to a series of appeals in state and federal courts. The US Supreme Court is the last resort for death row inmates, although it hears only a few death penalty cases each year. In addition to the appeals process, a state's governor or other body can grant clemency to a person on death row, postponing an execution for a period of time to allow further review of the case. A governor may also commute a death sentence to a lesser penalty such as life in prison without parole.

A lengthy appeals process provided the necessary checks and balances to prevent the wrongful execution of sixty-four-year-old Glenn Ford in Louisiana. After nearly thirty years on death row in a

> "Can we countenance a system that can't tell the difference between the innocent and the guilty?"[39]
>
> — Diann Rust-Tierney, executive director of the National Coalition Against the Death Penalty.

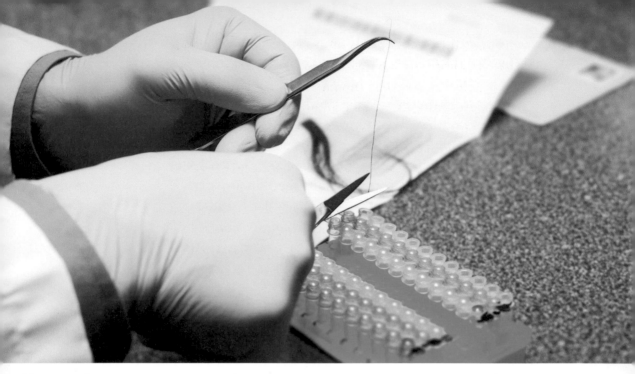

Hair samples (pictured above) are one of the more common bodily parts where DNA can be located and extracted for purpose of identification in criminal inquiries.

Louisiana state prison, in 2014 Ford was exonerated of murder and released from prison. A Louisiana jury had sentenced him to death after convicting him of first-degree murder in the 1983 killing of Isadore Rozeman, a Shreveport jeweler and watchmaker. Both during and after the trial Ford insisted that he was innocent of the crime. His lawyers fought the conviction through the appeals process over the next three decades. Eventually, new information surfaced that supported Ford's claim he was not present at the murder scene or involved in Rozeman's death. In 2013 prosecutors received information from a confidential informant that another individual was responsible for Rozeman's death. The state and Ford's legal counsel filed motions to vacate his conviction and sentence, which the court granted in 2014. In Ford's case the legal system's checks and balances worked to prevent an innocent man from being wrongly executed.

Improving Investigations Prevents Wrongful Convictions

Police and prosecutors are increasingly engaged in ensuring wrongful convictions do not occur. Prosecutors and investigators are using improved forensic tools and procedures to better link the right suspect to a crime. In 2013 the International Association of Chiefs of Police (IACP) called for police departments around the country to make changes in the way they conduct investigations in order to prevent wrongful convictions. In a joint effort with the Justice Department and the Innocence Project, the IACP endorsed thirty recommendations for changes in how police conduct photo line-ups, videotape witness interviews, and corroborate information obtained from informants. The IACP also called for police departments to create formal procedures for reviewing flawed cases and claims of innocence. "At the end of the day, the goal is to reduce the number of persons who are wrongfully convicted," says Walter A. McNeil, a police chief in Quincy, Florida, and past president of the IACP. "What we are trying to say in this report is, it's worth it for all of us, particularly law enforcement, to continue to evaluate, slow down, and get the right person."[41]

Because eyewitness misidentification is a significant factor in wrongful arrest and convictions, many police departments have implemented procedures to reduce the chance of error. According to the Innocence Project, eyewitness misidentifications played a role in the majority of more than three hundred convictions that were later overturned because of DNA evidence since 1989. To reduce potential sources of error or bias some police departments conduct blind lineups, where the police officer who shows photographs to a witness does not know who the suspect is. This prevents the officer from unknowingly or purposely signaling to the witness which photo is of the main suspect. Other agencies show witnesses photographs of potential suspects one at a time rather than in a group, which has been shown to reduce witness errors. Nearly ten states and several large city police departments such as Dallas and Baltimore have implemented blind and sequential policies for witness identification. In addition, more than twenty states record witness interrogations, and an additional 850 agencies voluntarily record interrogations to ensure that officers conduct the interviews according to protocol and thereby reduce the chance of mistakes. "We all support these reforms because they protect the innocent and enhance the ability of law enforcement to catch the guilty,"[42] says Barry Scheck, cofounder of the Innocence Project.

A forensic technician examines evidence at a crime scene. Over the last thirty years, advances in forensic science have significantly raised the level of criminal investigations by developing such reliable identification techniques as DNA testing.

DNA Testing

One of the most significant advances in criminal investigations is the use of DNA technology to link a suspect to a crime scene. Blood, hair, and other body substances found at a crime scene can identify a suspect. Every cell in the human body holds DNA, and the DNA sequence for every person is unique. Only identical twins have the same DNA. Investigators can compare DNA at a crime scene to DNA from a suspect. If it matches, the investigators have linked the suspect to the crime scene. DNA technology is a reliable tool that is widely used by police, prosecutors, defense attorneys, and courts.

DNA evidence can also exclude a person who is suspected of committing a crime and exonerate an individual who has been wrongfully convicted. In some cases, a defendant was convicted before DNA technology was available. Other times, DNA evidence surfaces after trial. The latter occurred in the case of Clemente Javier Aguirre-Jarquin, who had been sentenced to death for the 2004 murders of Cheryl Williams and Carol Bareis in Florida. In 2013 DNA testing confirmed Aguirre's innocence. In the early stages of the investigation he had told the police he knew nothing about the murders. He later admitted that he had found the women's bodies, panicked, and gone home. The prosecution presented limited DNA evidence at trial that showed the victims' blood on Aguirre's clothes, shoes, and a knife. No one tested more than 150 bloodstains photographed and swabbed at the crime scene. In 2011 Aguirre's new legal team, working with the Innocence Project, asked for DNA testing of the crime scene evidence. None of the test results matched Aguirre; however, several stains matched victim Cheryl Williams's daughter Samantha Williams who had a history of mental illness. "Tragically Mr. Aguirre's lawyer never requested the DNA testing that could have proven that he was innocent as he always maintained," says Nina Morrison, a senior staff attorney with the Innocence Project. "But new DNA testing on multiple pieces of evidence now confirms that Mr. Aguirre was telling the truth all along, and he shouldn't have to spend another day waiting to be put to death for a crime he didn't commit."[43] Aguirre's legal team has appealed to the Florida courts asking them to set aside the verdict in light of the new DNA evidence.

According to the Innocence Project, all fifty states have laws permitting inmates to access DNA testing to prove their innocence. In practice this can be difficult because many of the laws place limits on an inmate's access to this type of testing. In some cases courts deny motions for DNA testing even if the test could confirm guilt or exonerate an inmate before he or she is wrongfully executed.

A Shadow of Doubt

Recent exonerations of death row inmates have brought the issue of innocence and the death penalty to the forefront of the death penalty debate. Although new investigative procedures and better forensic testing can help investigators learn more about crimes than ever before, some people are still being wrongfully convicted of crimes. When this mistake occurs in a death penalty case, the stakes are extraordinarily high. For some, the execution of even one innocent person is the ultimate injustice. For this reason they believe the death penalty should be repealed across the United States. For others, ensuring the guilty are sufficiently punished is a primary concern, and the rare wrongful execution is an acceptable risk.

Facts

- Since 1976, 274 clemencies have been granted to death row inmates in the United States, according to the Death Penalty Information Center.

- Only the president has the power to grant a pardon for federal death row inmates.

- Since 1973 over 140 people have been released from death row with evidence of their innocence, according to the Death Penalty Information Center.

- There have been 316 post-conviction DNA exonerations in the United States, according to the Innocence Project.

- The Innocent Project reports that false confessions and incriminating statements lead to wrongful convictions in approximately 25 percent of cases.

- Informants contributed to wrongful convictions in 18 percent of cases, as reported by the Innocence Project.

Is the Death Penalty Applied Fairly?

Where the death penalty is concerned, all capital murder cases are not created equal. In one case, Ohio executed Clarence Carter in 2011 for the murder of a fellow prison inmate in 1989. At the time, Carter was in jail awaiting sentencing on an aggravated murder charge. The state's director of prisons urged the governor to spare Carter's life, saying the killing resulted during a fight between inmates. Prison officials found no evidence that the killing was planned. The governor declined to stay the execution, and Carter was put to death on April 12, 2011.

In a different case, in 2005, a Georgia jury sentenced Eric Rudolph to life in prison without chance of parole after he admitted to killing two people and injuring 150 others through a series of bombings. Rudolph set off bombs at the site of the Atlanta Summer Olympics in 1996, at an Atlanta area gay nightclub and an abortion clinic in 1997, and at an abortion clinic in Birmingham, Alabama, in 1998. Prosecutors agreed to a plea deal that spared Rudolph's life in exchange for information about where he had hidden 250 pounds of dynamite in the North Carolina mountains. Rudolph avoided the death penalty even though his crimes were premeditated and far larger in scope than Carter's crime.

These two cases illustrate the uneven application of the death penalty from one state to the next—and sometimes even within states. In part this is a result of the structure of the justice system in the United States. In this country states determine many of their own laws rather than operating under laws dictated by the federal government. This is true in areas other than death penalty cases, but when it involves such cases the result can be hugely problematic. A person who is convicted of capital murder in a death penalty state is at a distinct, and some would say unfair, disadvantage compared with someone who commits a similar crime in a non–death penalty state.

Many factors determine who is sentenced to death and who is executed in the United States. In addition to the severity of the crime and guilt of the defendant, arbitrary factors such as location of the crime, race of the defendant and victim, and quality of legal representation can influence the outcome of a case and its resulting punishment. "Both our general prison population and death row contain dangerous individuals convicted of serious crimes. But it would be hard to predict whether an inmate ended up on death row or in the general prison population if you were to examine only the facts of the crime. It would be even harder to foresee who would eventually be executed,"[44] says Richard C. Dieter.

Application of the Death Penalty

When reviewing the details of the cases that receive the death penalty, it becomes apparent that factors other than the severity of the crime and the responsibility of the defendant influence the application of the death penalty. A study in 2013 by Raymond Paternoster, a criminologist at the University of Maryland, reported that black defendants facing trial in Houston, Texas, were three times as likely to face a possible death sentence as were white defendants. Paternoster's study was commissioned by the defense team of Duane Buck, a current death row inmate in Texas.

The findings in the Houston study are one example of how the death penalty can be unfairly applied to defendants and cases across the country. "Whether or not one receives the death penalty depends upon the discretion of the prosecutor who initiates the proceeding, the competence of counsel who represents the defendant, the race of the victim, the race of the defendant, the make-up of the jury, the attitude of the judge, and the attitude and make-up of the appellate courts that review the verdict,"[45] says H. Lee Sarokin, retired judge of the US Court of Appeals for the Third Circuit.

Location

Where a defendant faces trial can mean the difference between life and death. A defendant can be sentenced to death in one state but given a prison sentence for a similar crime in another state. This is partly because states make their own laws. In some states the death penalty is permissible for certain crimes; in other states it is not. As of April 2014 thirty-two states, the federal government, and the US military had the death penalty. However, defendants in some states are more likely to receive the death penalty than in other states. Since the US Supreme Court reinstated the death penalty in 1976, 82 percent of all executions have taken place in three states: Texas, Virginia, and Oklahoma. These states have carried out hundreds of executions. Other death penalty states averaged fewer than one execution per year.

Even within a single state, there are variations in the application of the death penalty. A single county may produce hundreds of death sentences, while another county in the same state may produce few or no death sentences. "In almost all states, the decision to seek the death penalty is not made by a central state entity that evaluates the relative severity of committed homicides; rather, the charging decision is left to the discretion of the district attorney of each county. Prosecutors differ widely on what they consider to be the worst cases, and even on whether the death penalty should be sought at all. A defendant's chances of being sentenced to death may vary greatly depending on which side of the county line he committed a murder,"[46] says Dieter. For example, in Ohio, offenders charged with a capital crime in Cuyahoga County (Cleveland) received a death sentence 8 percent of the time. In contrast, in Ohio's Hamilton County (Cincinnati), 43 percent of offenders charged with capital crimes were sentenced to death.

A 2011 study by Robert J. Smith, professor at DePaul

States with and Without the Death Penalty

Beginning with Michigan in 1846, eighteen states have legally abolished the death penalty. In those states with the death penalty, the majority employ lethal injection while some even allow the condemned prisoner to select death by firing squad.

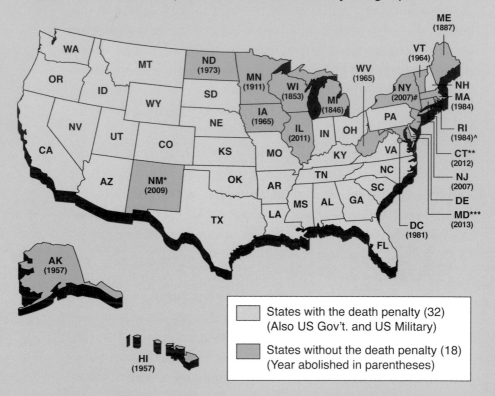

States with the death penalty (32)
(Also US Gov't. and US Military)

States without the death penalty (18)
(Year abolished in parentheses)

* In March 2009, New Mexico voted to abolish the death penalty. However, the repeal was not retroactive, leaving two people on the state's death row.

** In April 2012, Connecticut voted to abolish the death penalty. However, the repeal was not retroactive, leaving 11 people on the state's death row.

*** In May, 2013, Maryland abolished the death penalty. However, the repeal was not retroactive, leaving 5 people on the state's death row.

^ In 1979, the Supreme Court of Rhode Island held that a statute making a death sentence mandatory for someone who killed a fellow prisoner was unconstitutional. The legislature removed the statute in 1984.

In 2004, the New York Court of Appeals held that a portion of the state's death penalty law was unconstitutional. In 2007, it ruled that its prior holding applied to the last remaining person on the state's death row. The legislature has voted down attempts to restore the statute.

University College of Law, examined use of the death penalty in counties across the United States. The study found the majority of death sentences were handed down in only a small number of counties. Smith reported that the death sentences that resulted in executions between 2004 and 2009 came from less than 1 percent of US counties. He noted, "There is nothing to suggest that the murders committed in those active death-sentencing counties are more heinous than murders committed in other counties. Nor is there evidence to suggest that the offenders in those counties are more incorrigible than those who commit crimes in other counties."[47] Smith concluded that the disparity in sentencing based on geography might allow a challenge to the constitutionality of the death penalty under the Eighth Amendment.

Quality of Legal Representation

The quality of the defense team can also impact whether or not a defendant receives a death sentence. The number of attorneys assigned to a case, their experience in capital cases, and the funding available to pay for defense investigators and experts can affect whether a defendant receives the death penalty or a prison sentence. Across the country many defendants in capital cases cannot afford to hire their own lawyers. Instead, the jurisdiction provides them with a lawyer. In many cases the state-provided defense lawyers are overworked, underpaid, or lack the trial experience needed in death penalty cases. In some cases the appointed defense lawyers were unprepared for the sentencing part of the trial. Other times appointed lawyers have been grossly inadequate, sleeping through parts of the trial or arriving in court after drinking alcohol.

The difference in representation continues when a defendant appeals a death sentence. There are no national standards for appeals lawyers. Affluent defendants can hire their own legal teams. Others are left to rely on public defenders, if available. States are not required to provide attorneys for death row inmates throughout the appeals process. Some states have public defender offices dedicated to capital cases.

"There is nothing to suggest that the murders committed in those active death-sentencing counties are more heinous than murders committed in other counties."[47]

— Robert J. Smith, professor at DePaul University College of Law.

Paying for the Death Penalty

Sometimes whether a prosecutor seeks the death penalty in a capital case depends on cost and the county resources. Capital murder cases that might lead to a death penalty sentence are very expensive because they are often longer and more complex than other cases. Jurisdictions must pay additional costs for public defenders, prosecutors, trial experts, jury selection, and court costs. Death penalty cases are also entitled to a series of appeals, the costs of which are paid by the jurisdiction and its taxpayers.

In some counties prosecutors may choose not to seek the death penalty, in part because the county cannot pay for it. Like it or not, says Wharton County, Texas, district attorney Josh McCown, this is the reality district attorneys face when deciding whether to pursue the death penalty. "This is one of those things a district attorney doesn't like to talk about. You don't want to think that you're letting money come into play. You ought to consider the facts of a case and make your decisions in a vacuum. In a perfect world, that's the way you do it. But in a county this size you have to consider the level of expertise, the financial resources. If you don't, you're stupid. This is not a perfect system or a perfect world," says McCown.

Quoted in Allan Turner, "Death Penalty May Carry Heavy Price for Austin Co.," *Houston Chronicle*, October 4, 2009. www.chron.com.

Defendants in other states are left without representation during parts of the appeal process.

The case of Leroy White, executed in Alabama in 2011, is an example of what can happen when a death row inmate does not have the means to hire lawyers who are experienced in capital murder and death penalty cases. Before White's trial in connection with the 1988 murder of his wife, prosecutors had offered him a plea bargain. By accepting the plea White would have received a sentence of life in prison without parole. However, he turned it down after his lawyer mistakenly told him that he could not be convicted of capital murder or receive a death sentence. At the close of the trial the jury recommended a life sentence, but the judge overturned the jury's recommendation and sentenced White to die. White's representation suffered again during his appeal when one of his lawyers missed an appeal deadline and then withdrew from the case without notifying his client. Although the lawyer was experienced in tax and corporate law, he had never been in a courtroom before handling White's case. The missed deadline hastened White's execution date.

A mistake by Alabama death row inmate Ronald B. Smith's lawyer cost him a chance to challenge his conviction and death sentence. In December 2013 a federal appeals court in Atlanta ruled that Smith could not challenge his conviction and death sentence because he had not properly filed a document by a certain deadline. The court said Smith's lawyer did not pay a $154 filing fee or file a motion to establish that his client was indigent and therefore could not afford the fee and would need a waiver. At the time he made the filing mistake in 2001, Smith's lawyer had been arrested twice for public intoxication and drug possession, according to a report by the *New York Times*. According to a sworn statement from the lawyer's legal assistant, the lawyer often arrived at work intoxicated and sometimes had to be awakened at home and taken to court appearances. Over the next year the lawyer was charged with drug possession again, declared bankruptcy, and committed suicide in 2002. When Smith's case reached the appellate court and was turned down for consideration, at least one judge dissented. In her dissenting opinion, appeals court Judge Rosemary Barkett said she believed Smith should be allowed to make his case in federal court. "It is unjust and inequitable," she wrote, "to require death row inmates to suffer the consequences of their attorneys' negligence."[48] As of mid-2014 Smith still sits on Alabama's death row.

Racial Bias

Race can also influence who gets the death penalty—both the race of the defendant and the race of the victim. Multiple studies have shown a connection between race and the death penalty. One of the most comprehensive and well-known studies of race and the death penalty was published by University of Iowa law professor David Baldus and colleagues in 1983. They studied over two thousand potential death penalty cases in Georgia and compared variables that might influence whether a defendant would receive a death sentence. Baldus's study found that black defendants were 1.7 times more likely to receive the death penalty than white defendants. He also found murderers of white victims were 4.3 times more likely to receive the death penalty than cases involving black victims.

The Baldus study was reviewed in the Supreme Court's 1987 decision in *McCleskey v. Kemp*. In the case, Warren McCleskey, an African American, was sentenced to death for the murder of a white Atlanta police officer. McCleskey's legal team argued the

Awaiting death by electrocution for the fatal shooting of an off-duty policeman, Warren McCleskey appealed to the US Supreme Court to have his sentence reduced to life imprisonment. The court ruled to uphold the sentence despite defense arguments that the sentence was racially motivated. He was executed in September 1991.

Baldus study showed his death sentence was unjustly influenced by racial bias. The Supreme Court eventually ruled in a 5–4 decision to uphold McCleskey's death sentence. The justices said general patterns of discrimination noted in the study were not enough to prove racial discrimination in McCleskey's specific case. Justice Brennan dissented from the majority opinion and wrote, "That a decision to impose the death penalty could be influenced by race is a particularly repugnant prospect, and evidence that race may play even a modest role in levying a death sentence should be enough to characterize that sentence as 'cruel and unusual.'"[49]

In the years since the Baldus study, other studies have also found a racial bias in the death penalty. A 2014 study by Katherine Beckett, a professor at the University of Washington, found jurors in Washington were three times more likely to recommend the death penalty for a black defendant than a white defendant in a similar case. Beckett's study reviewed 285 cases involving defendants who were convicted of aggravated murder. The study was commissioned by death row attorneys Lila Silverstein and Neil Fox. They plan to use the report's findings in an appeal for death row inmate Allen Eugene Gregory, a black man convicted of raping and murdering a white woman in Pierce County, Washington, in 1996. "Washington is not a state that tolerates discrimination, even when it doesn't involve a matter of life and death. We can't be putting people to death based on their race,"[50] says Silverstein

"We can't be putting people to death based on their race."[50]

— Lila Silverstein, a death row attorney in Washington.

The race of the victim can also influence death penalty sentences. A 2011 study found that in parts of North Carolina the chances of receiving a death sentence were 2.6 times higher for defendants accused of killing a white victim than those accused of killing a black victim. That study was conducted by Michael Radelet, a sociology professor at the University of Colorado at Boulder and a leading authority on the death penalty, and Glenn Pierce, a research scientist in the School of Criminology and Criminal Justice at Northeastern University in Boston. Said Radelet: "It's just kind of baffling that, in this day and age, race matters."[51]

Racial Justice Act

At least one state tried to take steps to reduce racial bias in death penalty cases. North Carolina legislators passed that state's Racial Justice Act in 2009. The act stated that if race is found to be a significant factor in applying the death penalty, then the death sentence will be commuted to a sentence of life without parole. The act allowed defendants to challenge their sentence based on three points—the death penalty was more likely because of the defendant's race, the death penalty was more likely because of the victim's race, and the death penalty was more likely because jury selection in the case was racially biased. The act allowed inmates to use state and county statistics and other material to argue race was a factor in their sentencing.

After the passage of the Racial Justice Act, most North Carolina death row inmates challenged their sentences. One inmate, thirty-eight-year-old Marcus Robinson, received the death penalty for the 1991 kidnapping and murder of a seventeen-year-old boy. At Robinson's trial the prosecution removed half of all qualified African American jurors from serving on the jury but removed only 15 percent of white jurors. As a result, the jury in Robinson's case included nine whites, two blacks and one Native American, even though the county from which the jury was selected was 40 percent black. In the challenge allowed under the act, Robinson's legal team argued race was a significant factor during jury selection for his trial. In 2012 a judge agreed and found intentional and systemic discrimination by state prosecutors against potential African American jurors. Robinson's sentence was commuted to life in prison without parole.

As more inmates appealed their death sentences, some North Carolina lawmakers feared the act was being used to essentially do away with the death penalty in the state rather than for its true purpose of eliminating racial bias in these cases. "Nearly every person on death row, regardless of race, has appealed their death sentence under the Racial Justice Act," says Governor Pat McCrory in a 2013 statement. "The state's district attorneys are nearly unanimous in their bipartisan conclusion that the Racial Justice Act cre-

Gender and the Death Penalty

As of January 1, 2013, death rows in the United States included sixty-three women, or about 2 percent of the total death row population. A 2011 study concludes that the low number of women on California's death row results from gender bias. That study was conducted by Steven Shatz, a professor at the University of San Francisco Law School, and Naomi Shatz of the New York Civil Liberties Union. For their study the researchers reviewed thirteen hundred murder cases in California and found that women convicted of murder were far less likely than men to be sentenced to death. In addition, defendants who killed female victims were far more likely to be sentenced to death than those whose victims were men.

The study authors concluded, "The present study confirms what earlier studies have shown: that the death penalty is imposed on women relatively infrequently and that it is disproportionately imposed for the killing of women. Thus, the death penalty . . . appears to be applied in accordance with stereotypes about women's innate abilities, their roles in society, and their capacity for violence. Far from being gender neutral, the California death penalty seems to allow prejudices and stereotypes about violence and gender, chivalric values, to determine who lives and who dies."

Quoted in Steven F. Shatz and Naomi R. Shatz, "Chivalry Is Not Dead: Murder, Gender, and the Death Penalty," University of San Francisco Law School, 2011.

ated a judicial loophole to avoid the death penalty and not a path to justice."[52] In light of these concerns, North Carolina legislators repealed the state's Racial Justice Act in 2013.

The repeal brought a mixed response among North Carolinians. Those who agree with the repeal said the act denied justice to victims and was flawed. "It tries to put a carte blanche solution on the problem," says state representative Tim Moore. "A white supremacist who murdered an African-American could argue he was a victim of racism if blacks were on the jury."[53] For others, the repeal was a step backward for ending racial bias in the justice system and on death row. "It's incredibly sad," says state representative Rick Glazier, a supporter of the act. "If you can't face up to your history and make sure it's not repeated, it lends itself to being repeated."[54]

Suspending the Death Penalty

The controversy over the fair application of the death penalty has led to calls for its repeal. In 2009 the American Law Institute (ALI), an organization of the country's leading jurists and legal scholars, voted to rescind the parts of its Model Penal Code that deal with the death penalty. The code was developed by the ALI to help states in developing their own laws. The ALI determined that the death penalty failed to punish only the worst offenders.

On February 11, 2014, Washington governor Jay Inslee announced the suspension of the death penalty in his state. He claimed that equal justice under the law was ill-served by capital punishment and that he would maintain his policy as long as he remained governor.

The general public is also concerned with how the death penalty is being applied. The arbitrariness of sentences that decide who lives and who dies concerns a majority of Americans. A 2010 national poll conducted by Lake Research Partners found that two-thirds of respondents would prefer an alternative to the death penalty in capital murder cases. Many cited the unfairness in sentencing as a top concern. In addition, 69 percent of respondents said they disagreed with the death penalty because it was applied unevenly.

Some states have recently tried to address these concerns. In 2014 Governor Jay Inslee of Washington announced a moratorium on the death penalty in his state. Inslee said that after months of research on current cases, discussion with prosecutors, police, and victims' families, he concluded that the death penalty was being applied inconsistently and unequally in the state. "Equal justice under the law is the state's primary responsibility," says Inslee. "I'm not convinced equal justice is being served."[55] Inslee said whether a defendant was sentenced to death sometimes depended on the county where the crime was committed and how much money was available for the county to prosecute the case. While the moratorium does not commute the sentences of the nine inmates currently on Washington's death row, Inslee said he will grant reprieves to prevent future executions. National Association for the Advancement of Colored People (NAACP) criminal justice director Niaz Kasravi applauded the governor's action. "The system of capital punishment is one that is discriminatory against people of color and the poor—it is riddled with inconsistencies and risks innocent lives, and it's a fiscally wasteful practice with no deterrent effect on crime," says Kasravi. "By issuing a moratorium on the death penalty, Gov. Inslee today took a very important step towards fixing Washington's criminal justice system."[56]

Working to Make the System Fair

Most people who follow the history of the death penalty in the United States acknowledge that it has at times been applied unfairly, especially where nonwhite defendants are concerned. However, supporters argue that the legal system is working to improve how death sentences are given. Since the 1960s there has been increasing participation by minorities in the legal system. More minorities are serving as jurors, lawyers, judges, and in law enforcement. With more participation by people of all races and backgrounds, the legal system will become fairer, ensuring the death penalty is applied fairly to all.

Death penalty supporters point out that although racial bias exists, it has decreased over time. Between 1930 and 1967, 54 percent of inmates executed were African American. Since 1977 the racial makeup of executions has shifted toward the general US population's racial distribution. Since 1977, 56 percent of those executed have been white, while 35 percent have been black, and 9 percent Latino.

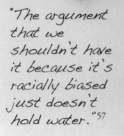

Death penalty supporters also argue that a general racial bias should not be grounds for dismissing a defendant's death sentence. Instead, they say that the merits of each case should be reviewed. In 2013 a Connecticut judge rejected a claim by five convicted murderers that the state's death penalty law was racially biased. In his decision Judge Samuel J. Sferrazza said the defendants did not prove any racial, ethical, or geographical bias in the state's application of the death penalty in their cases. Chief state's attorney Kevin Kane said the defendants did not bring specific evidence to support their claim of bias as it applied to their cases. "The argument that we shouldn't have it [the death penalty] because it's racially biased just doesn't hold water,"[57] he says.

An Imperfect System

Most people agree that when a defendant's life is at stake, the criminal justice system should be as fair as possible and free from bias. Although improvements have been made to put all defendants on a level playing field, there are still problems in the criminal justice system and death penalty trials that may affect whether a defendant lives or dies. Racial bias, differences in legal representation, and even the location of the trial can all impact a defendant's sentence. Many believe more work needs to be done to eliminate any bias from the death penalty process. "I want to acknowledge that there are many good protections built into Washington State's death penalty law," says Inslee. "But there have been too many doubts raised about capital punishment. There are too many flaws in the system. And when the ultimate decision is death, there is too much at stake to accept an imperfect system."[58]

Facts

- In murder cases that resulted in an execution, over 75 percent of victims were white, while only 50 percent of all murder victims are white, according to the Death Penalty Information Center (DPIC).

- In Maryland, an average death penalty case resulting in a death sentence costs approximately $3 million, reports the Urban Institute Justice Policy Center.

- A 2011 Pew Research report found that 27 percent of those who oppose the death penalty said the imperfect nature of the justice system was their reason.

- As of April 2014 approximately 42 percent of death row inmates were black and 43 percent of inmates were white, according to the Death Penalty Information Center.

- The DPIC reports that there were 290 cases in which a defendant was executed for the murder of a person of a different race between 1976 and April 24, 2014. Of those cases, 270 of them involved a black defendant and a white victim. In only 20 cases, a white defendant was executed for the murder of a black victim.

CHAPTER FIVE

Are Death Penalty Methods Constitutional?

I n January 2014 Dennis McGuire was executed by lethal injection at the Southern Ohio Correctional Facility near Lucasville, Ohio. The execution process began, as many have in Ohio, with the insertion of intravenous needles in McGuire's arms. He made a brief statement, apologizing to the victim's family and telling his family that he loved them. Around 10:30 a.m. the lethal injection chemicals began to flow into McGuire's veins. Five minutes later McGuire started to struggle in his restraints. He repeatedly gasped for air. For about ten minutes McGuire snorted and choked, his chest and stomach heaved, and his hand clenched into a fist. Eventually McGuire gasped two last times and was still. More than twenty minutes after the execution began he was pronounced dead.

McGuire was put to death with a combination of intravenous drugs that had never been used before for lethal injection. Ohio prison officials had chosen to use the new combination of drugs because the drugs used in prior executions were unavailable. McGuire's lawyers had argued prior to the execution that the new drug combination was unproven and could cause agony and terror before killing him. Allen Bohnert, one of McGuire's public defenders, said the execution was agonizing and a failed experiment. "The people of the state of Ohio should be appalled by what was done in their name,"[59] says Bohnert. An anti–death penalty group,

Ohioans to Stop Executions, called for an immediate moratorium on the death penalty in the state.

After McGuire's execution his family announced they would file a lawsuit over his death. "I can't think of any other way to describe it than torture,"[60] daughter Amber McGuire said in a statement. John Paul Rion, a lawyer representing the McGuire family in their lawsuit, said that the execution violated McGuire's constitutional protection against cruel and unusual punishment.

Others had less sympathy for the way in which McGuire died. Ohio's assistant attorney general Thomas Madden argued that McGuire was not entitled to a pain-free execution under the Constitution. The family of McGuire's victim, Joy Stewart, was also present. They watched the execution in silence. McGuire was convicted of raping Stewart in 1989. According to court records, he choked her and slashed her throat, killing her and her thirty-week-old fetus. After the execution a member of Stewart's family issued a statement, saying, "There has been a lot of controversy regarding the drugs that are to be used in his execution, concern that he might feel terror, that he might suffer. As I recall the events preceding her death . . . I know she suffered terror and pain. He is being treated far more humanely than he treated her."[61]

The controversy over McGuire's execution is part of a larger debate over the methods used to carry out the death penalty in the United States. While most people want to see justice served when heinous crimes are committed, even those who support the death penalty become concerned when executions appear to cause pain and suffering. At what point does acceptable pain and suffering cross the line to become cruel and unusual punishment?

Execution Methods

Over the years several methods of execution have been used in the United States. Through the nineteenth century prisoners were most commonly executed by hanging. Although it sounds simple, hanging was often carried out improperly. If the drop was too short, the prisoner died a slow death by strangulation. If the drop was too long, the prisoner's head would be ripped off as he or she fell. Some jurisdictions employed firing squads to administer the

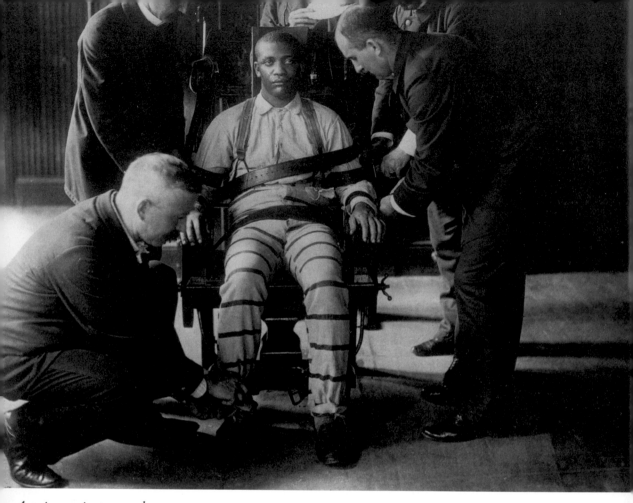

death penalty. The prisoner was strapped to a chair. A hood was placed over his or her head and a target pinned to the chest. Five shooters, including one armed with blanks, took aim and fired. In this way, no one knew who fired the fatal shot.

In the late 1800s Thomas Edison's work with electricity spurred the development of the electric chair, which used alternating electrical current to put a prisoner to death. Prisoners were strapped to the electric chair, and electrodes were attached to the head and legs. In New York in 1890 convicted murderer William Kemmler was the first person to be put to death via the electric chair. By the twentieth century electrocution became the most widely used method of execution. Electrocution had many flaws. It could set the prisoner on fire and cause extreme pain. Many times electrocution witnesses reported seeing smoke rising from the head of the prisoner and smelling the odor of burning flesh. Prisoners strained and jolted as the current flowed through their bodies. No one knew how long the electrocuted person remained conscious during the process.

In the search for a more humane method of execution, some states turned to the gas chamber. This method required the prisoner to be strapped to a chair with a container of sulfuric acid placed underneath the chair. After the gas chamber was sealed, the executioner flicked a switch to release cyanide into the sulfuric acid, forming a lethal gas. Although proponents of the gas chamber said that death induced in this manner would be quick and painless, many execution witnesses reported otherwise.

Convicted murderer Donald Harding was executed in Arizona's gas chamber in 1992. A witness described the execution as follows:

> When the fumes enveloped Don's head he took a quick breath. . . . His face was red and contorted as if he were attempting to fight through tremendous pain. His mouth was pursed shut and his jaw was clenched tight. Don then took several more quick gulps of the fumes. At this point Don's body started convulsing violently. . . . His face and body turned a deep red and the veins in his temple and neck began to bulge until I thought they might explode. After about a minute Don's face leaned partially forward but he was still conscious. Every few seconds he continued to gulp. He was shuddering uncontrollably and his body was racked with spasms. His head continued to snap back His hands were clenched. After several more minutes, the most violent of the convulsions subsided. At this time the muscles along Don's left arm and back began twitching in a wave-like motion under his skin.[62]

Harding's death took ten minutes and thirty-one seconds.

The Switch to Lethal Injection

Looking for a more humane way to carry out the death penalty, an Oklahoma medical examiner named Jay Chapman proposed

Compounding Pharmacies

As prisons have had more difficulty obtaining the drugs used in lethal injections, some have turned to compounding pharmacies to provide execution drugs. Compounding pharmacies combine, mix, or alter drugs. They are typically used to meet the specific needs of a patient. For example, a compounding pharmacy might alter a drug to remove an inactive ingredient for a patient with allergies. The pharmacy might also take a traditional pill-form medication and put it into a liquid form for a child patient. Some compounding pharmacies make drugs that are copies or near copies of commercially available drugs.

Compounding pharmacies are not subjected to the same federal regulations and testing as larger drug manufacturers. As a result, there are concerns about the safety and efficacy of some of the drugs they produce. For lethal injection drugs supplied by compounding pharmacies, the concern is that they may include contaminants that cause substantial pain.

in 1977 that death row inmates be executed using a combination of three drugs injected intravenously. The three drugs would be administered in a specific sequence. First a barbiturate would be injected to anesthetize the prisoner. Then a drug called pancuronium bromide would be injected to paralyze the prisoner and stop his or her breathing. Finally, a third drug, potassium chloride, would be administered to stop the prisoner's heart.

Chapman's idea was well received. It did not have the drawbacks of electrocution and gassing, and because prisoners would be paralyzed during the procedure, they would not squirm and cry out as they died. The Oklahoma state legislature immediately approved Chapman's idea. Other states also quickly adopted lethal injection as an approved method of execution. In 1982 Texas became the first state to use lethal injection, executing forty-year-old Charles Brooks for the murder of a Fort Worth mechanic in 1976.

Although other types of executions can still be carried out in some states, lethal injection has become the standard method of execution in the United States. Lethal injection is intended to give states a more humane way to execute death row inmates. In some jurisdictions prisoners are able to choose their method of execution; most select lethal injection. According to the Death Penalty Information Center, 1,203 out of 1,378 executions between 1976 and April 2014 were carried out through lethal injection.

The exact combination of lethal injection drugs can vary by state. Some states use a three-drug combination, while others use a two-drug combination or a single drug. The drugs are given to the prisoner in a specific sequence, says John DiCapua, an anesthesiologist at North Shore–LIJ Health system in Great Neck, New York. "The way a body dies [from lethal injection] is from lack of oxygen to the tissues, causing them to stop functioning,"[63] says DiCapua. DiCapua warns, however, that the drugs must be administered correctly in order for the execution to kill quickly and painlessly.

Botched Procedures

Many variables are involved in a lethal injection execution. The experience and training of the executioner varies from case to case. Often prison staff, not medical personnel, are responsible for inserting the needles, which can lead to complications and errors. In addition, because every prisoner is different, the doses of the drugs required for a lethal injection can vary. In some cases veins that are scarred from prior drug use can cause difficulty in administering the drugs.

With all of these variables it is not surprising that over the years there have been several cases of lethal injections taking longer or being more difficult to administer than expected. In some of these cases the prisoners have exhibited pain and distress for lengthy periods. In 2006 Angel Diaz was scheduled to die by lethal injection in Florida. Although the first injection was supposed make him unconscious, Diaz continued to move, squint, and grimace. A second dose was administered. Diaz took thirty-four minutes to die.

After the execution the medical examiner determined that prison officials had botched the execution by inserting the needle completely through Diaz's vein rather than into its center. This meant that the deadly dose went into the soft inner flesh of his arms instead of into the vein where it could be transported by the blood to his heart. The medical examiner found chemical burns on Diaz's arms, which suggested he felt significant pain during the procedure. A few days after Diaz's execution Florida governor Jeb Bush suspended all executions in the state and appointed a commission to study protocols of lethal injections. "These developments show that the current lethal-injection protocols pose an unacceptable risk of cruelty," says Jamie Fellner, director of US programs for Human Rights Watch. "The way states have been killing people for the last 30 years has yielded botched execution after botched execution."[64] In 2007 the commission recommended several procedural changes to Florida's lethal injection protocols to minimize the risk of botched executions.

Cruel and Unusual Punishment

Objectors point to botched executions as evidence that lethal injection drugs are a form of cruel and unusual punishment. According to Teresa Zimmers, a University of Miami Miller School of Medicine molecular biologist who has studied lethal injection, the drug often used to stop a prisoner's heart, potassium chloride, is extremely painful. In addition, it is unclear if the drugs used to render a prisoner unconscious are used in sufficient doses to eliminate pain or if they simply mask a prisoner's suffering from witnesses. Zimmers says lethal injections have not been tested adequately enough for officials to be certain they are not causing unnecessary pain and suffering. "There's no record of a medical or scientific inquiry into whether this would be the best method. And there isn't any medical evidence to support this approach," she says. "Part of the paradox is that it looks like a medical procedure, but it hasn't been rigorously tested. There are no controlled trials, data collection, analysis or peer review of the processes to determine whether it works the way it's been said to work."[65]

In 2009 Ohio death row inmate Rommel Broom suffered during an attempted lethal injection. Broom endured eighteen attempts by prison officials to find a vein. For over two hours these officials unsuccessfully tried to execute him. Eventually Ohio governor Ted Strickland ordered the execution to stop and granted Broom a one-week stay of execution so that doctors could be consulted. "Ohio's execution system is fundamentally flawed. If the state is going to take a person's life, they must ensure that it is done as humanely as possible," says ACLU counsel Carrie Davis. "With three botched executions in as many years, it's clear that the state must stop and review the system entirely before another person is put to death."[66] As of April 2014 Broom remained on Ohio's death row as the courts determined whether a second execution attempt would be constitutional.

Ongoing questions about how humane lethal injection is have led several states to suspend executions while state officials review the situation. "Lethal injection became the preferred method, because of the notion that it is easy and painless," says David Dow, a professor at the University of Houston Law Center and a death penalty opponent. "What has been revealed over the last several years is that it is neither."[67] In Maryland officials suspended the use of lethal injection while officials reviewed whether the procedure caused undue pain and whether prison staff were adequately trained to perform the procedure.

Supporters of the death penalty counter that the barbiturate and paralytic drugs used in lethal injections are used safely and effectively in thousands of anesthetics every day. In addition, supporters contend that convicted murderers are not entitled under the Constitution to pain-free executions. For those who hold this view, the pain or discomfort experienced during an execution do not justify stopping lethal injections. "I think most prosecutors feel the way I do—that it's an absurdity to hear that someone is in too much pain from having a needle stuck in their arm when we're talking about someone who's on death row for inflicting a great deal of pain,"

"Lethal injection became the preferred method, because of the notion that it is easy and painless. What has been revealed over the last several years is that it is neither."[67]

— David Dow, a professor at the University of Houston Law Center.

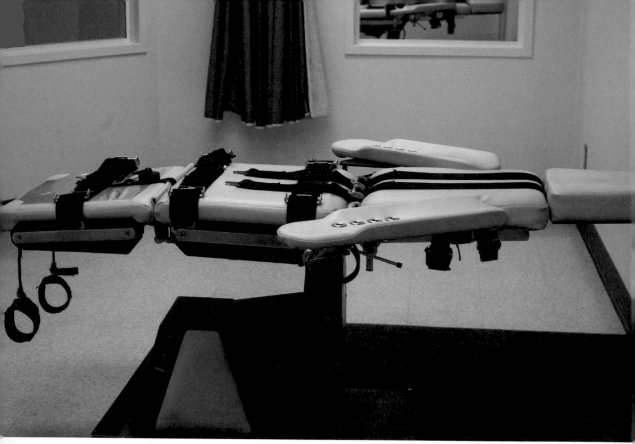

The injection table used at San Quentin State Prison in California. While proponents of death by lethal injection argue that it is the most humane method of execution, opponents cite executions that have gone badly and evidence by physiologists that enormous pain is associated with drugs frequently used in the procedure.

says Steven Stewart, the prosecuting attorney for Clark County, Indiana. "For a defendant to argue that it's cruel because they feel a little pain during the execution process is absurd."[68]

Constitutional Challenge—*Baze v. Rees*

Challenges to lethal injection are not new. In 2007 executions across the country were halted as several challenges to the lethal injection process were filed in court. These challenges asserted that it was a form of cruel and unusual punishment and a violation of the Eighth Amendment to the Constitution, which bans cruel and unusual punishment. Courts struggled with how to decide whether lethal injection violated the Eighth Amendment. Some courts used a standard of whether a procedure had a "substantial risk" of pain. Others looked to see if it had an "unnecessary risk" of pain or "excessive pain." The different standards led to differing opinions depending on the court hearing the case.

Finally in 2008 the US Supreme Court addressed the constitutionality of lethal injection in *Baze v. Rees*. Defendants Ralph Baze and Thomas C. Bowling were convicted of separate, unrelated double murders and sentenced to death. In their lawsuit the men claimed the existing lethal injection protocol violated the Eighth Amendment because it was likely to cause substantial pain and suffering. The protocol used a combination of three drugs to anesthetize, paralyze, and cause the heart to stop. The suit argued prisoners could regain consciousness during the procedure but remain paralyzed. If this were to happen they would probably feel pain when receiving the heart-stopping drug but be unable to tell prison officials.

On April 16, 2008, the Supreme Court ruled that Kentucky's three-drug lethal injection protocol was not cruel and unusual punishment under the Eighth Amendment. The court also said there was no constitutional right to a painless execution. The "Constitution does not demand the avoidance of all risk of pain in carrying out executions,"[69] said Chief Justice John Roberts. After the *Baze v. Rees* decision, some states resumed lethal injection executions.

> "For a defendant to argue that it's cruel because they feel a little pain during the execution process is absurd."[68]
>
> Steven Stewart, the prosecuting attorney for Clark County, Indiana.

Drug Shortages

More recently, prisons have faced a nationwide shortage of drugs used in lethal injection procedures. In 2011 the only American manufacturer of sodium thiopental—one of the key components of the three-drug lethal injection combination—stopped making the drug. States turned to European drug makers to obtain the drugs. Because many European countries do not have the death penalty, citizens of those countries objected to the export of their drugs for US executions. As a result, states have been forced to use other drugs.

Some states have turned to the drug pentobarbital. Pentobarbital is controversial because it is often poorly regulated during manufacturing, which can lead to contaminated batches that cause excruciating pain before death. Tanya Greene, an advocacy and policy counsel on criminal justice issues for the ACLU, says

Eyewitness to Electrocution

An unnamed eyewitness to the 1983 electrocution of John Evans in Alabama describes the horrifying event in detail:

At 8:30 p.m. the first jolt of 1900 volts of electricity passed through Mr. Evans' body. It lasted thirty seconds. Sparks and flames erupted . . . from the electrode tied to Mr. Evans' left leg. His body slammed against the straps holding him in the electric chair and his fist clenched permanently. The electrode apparently burst from the strap holding it in place. A large puff of grayish smoke and sparks poured out from under the hood that covered Mr. Evans' face. An overpowering stench of burnt flesh and clothing began pervading the witness room. Two doctors examined Mr. Evans and declared that he was not dead. The electrode on the left leg was re-fastened. . . . Mr. Evans was administered a second thirty second jolt of electricity. The stench of burning flesh was nauseating. More smoke emanated from his leg and head. Again, the doctors examined Mr. Evans. [They] reported that his heart was still beating, and that he was still alive. At that time, I asked the prison commissioner, who was communicating on an open telephone line to Governor George Wallace, to grant clemency on the grounds that Mr. Evans was being subjected to cruel and unusual punishment. The request . . . was denied. At 8:40 p.m., a third charge of electricity, thirty seconds in duration, was passed through Mr. Evans' body. At 8:44, the doctors pronounced him dead. The execution of John Evans took fourteen minutes.

Quoted in American Civil Liberties Union, "The Case Against the Death Penalty," December 11, 2012. www.aclu.org.

the use of pentobarbital in executions is unconstitutional because it violates the Eighth Amendment's protection against cruel and unusual punishment. Pentobarbital for lethal injection is "basically an experiment on human beings; the risk of extended, painful death is very high. The European manufacturer of pentobarbital objects to its use to kill and has stopped selling the drug to US states for use in executions,"[70] she says.

In January 2014 death row inmate Michael Lee Wilson was executed in Oklahoma using a mix of drugs that included pentobarbital. Execution witnesses reported that Wilson said, "I feel my whole body burning,"[71] during the execution. Civil rights groups have said that Wilson's case is further evidence that pentobarbital should be banned from use in executions.

In addition, when prisons use new combinations of drugs for lethal injections, experts say there is no way to know what will happen when they are administered. Some death row inmates in Missouri, Texas, and Oklahoma have sued to learn more about the drugs that will be used in their executions. To date, judges have denied these requests.

In April 2014 Oklahoma used a new combination of lethal injection drugs to execute convicted murderer Clayton Lockett. After Lockett was supposed to be made unconscious by the first in a three-drug combination, he began writhing, clenching his teeth, and straining to lift his head. Officials halted the execution, but Lockett died of an apparent heart attack forty-three minutes after the execution began. Afterward, Oklahoma governor Mary Fallin delayed the execution of a second death row inmate, Charles Warner, for fourteen days so the state could conduct an investigation into Lockett's execution. "We have a fundamental standard in this country that even when the death penalty is justified, it must be carried out humanely. And I think everyone would recognize that this case fell short of that standard,"[72] says press secretary Jay Carney in a White House statement after Lockett's execution.

"We have a fundamental standard in this country that even when the death penalty is justified, it must be carried out humanely."[72]

— Jay Carney, White House Press Secretary.

A Humane Execution

Although many Americans support the tough justice of the death penalty, most can agree that they do not want executions to be cruel or inhumane, even when putting to death people who have committed terrible crimes. Recent execution difficulties in Ohio and Oklahoma may prompt officials nationwide to look more closely at execution methods, with the goal of ensuring a humane execution for all death row inmates. Yet some experts, such as Douglas Berman, a capital punishment expert and law professor at Ohio State University, say finding an alternative everyone agrees is humane may be next to impossible. "I don't think that exists. And that's the challenge," says Berman. "It's not easy to kill someone in a way where no one is going to be upset about it."[73]

> "It's not easy to kill someone in a way where no one is going to be upset about it."[73]
>
> — Douglas Berman, a capital punishment expert and law professor at Ohio State University.

Facts

- The last execution by hanging took place in Delaware in 1996.

- In an electrocution a jolt of between five hundred and two thousand volts, which lasts for about thirty seconds, is given to the prisoner.

- The Supreme Court has never declared a method of execution unconstitutional on the grounds that it is cruel and unusual. Over the past 135 years it upheld the firing squad (1879), the electric chair (1890), and then lethal injection (2008).

- Lethal injection is the sole method of execution for US military capital crimes.

- Ronnie Lee Gardner was the last American killed by firing squad in Utah in 2010.

Source Notes

Introduction: Justice or Tragedy?

1. Quoted in Thanh Truong, "Two Versions of Justice in Troy Davis Case," NBC News, September 21, 2011. www.usnews.nbcnews.com.
2. Quoted in John Rudolf, "Troy Davis Executed: Controversially Convicted Inmate Maintains Innocence Until the End," *Huffington Post*, September 21, 2011. www.huffingtonpost.com.
3. Quoted in Truong, "Two Versions of Justice in Troy Davis Case."
4. Quoted in Kim Severson, "Davis Is Executed in Georgia," *New York Times*, September 21, 2011. www.nytimes.com.
5. Quoted in Rudolf, "Troy Davis Executed."
6. Quoted in Rudolf, "Troy Davis Executed."

Chapter One: What Are the Origins of the Death Penalty Controversy?

7. Quoted in The Death Penalty, "Constitutional Requirements." http://deathpenaltycurriculum.org.
8. United States Constitution, Eighth Amendment, Legal Information Institute, Cornell University Law School. www.law.cornell.edu.
9. United States Supreme Court, "*Furman v. Georgia*—Oral Argument," Oyez Project, January 17, 1972. www.oyez.org.
10. Legal Information Institute, Cornell University Law School, "*Furman v. Georgia*, United States Supreme Court, June 29, 1972." www.law.cornell.edu.
11. Quoted in Death Penalty Information Center, "U.S. Supreme Court: June 29 Marks 40th Anniversary of *Furman v. Georgia*," June 26, 2012. www.deathpenaltyinfo.org.
12. Quoted in Death Penalty Information Center, "U.S. Supreme Court: June 29 Marks 40th Anniversary of *Furman v. Georgia*."

13. Legal Information Institute, Cornell University Law School, "*Furman v. Georgia*, United States Supreme Court, June 29, 1972." www.law.cornell.edu.

14. United States Supreme Court, *Gregg v. Georgia*, July 2, 1976. http://caselaw.lp.findlaw.com.

Chapter Two: Is the Death Penalty Just Retribution for the Worst Crimes?

15. Quoted in Fox News.com, "Prosecutors Seek Death Penalty for Boston Marathon Bombing Suspect," January 30, 2014. www.foxnews.com.

16. Quoted in Catherine E. Shoichet, "For Boston Bombing Victims, Death Penalty Decision a 'Step Forward,'" CNN.com, January 30, 2014. www.cnn.com.

17. Quoted in Shoichet, "For Boston Bombing Victims, Death Penalty Decision a 'Step Forward.'"

18. Quoted in Brian MacQuarrie, "In *Globe* Poll, Most Favor Life Term for Dzhokhar Tsarnaev," *Boston Globe*, September 16, 2013. www.bostonglobe.com.

19. Quoted in Denise Lavoie, "US Prosecutors Seek Execution of Marathon Suspect," AP.org, January 30, 2014. http://bigstory.ap.org.

20. Jim Buchy, "Ohio's Death Penalty Brings Murderers to Justice: State Rep. Jim Buchy," Cleveland.com, February 23, 2014. www.cleveland.com.

21. Buchy, "Ohio's Death Penalty Brings Murderers to Justice."

22. George Brauchler, "Death Penalty Is a Tool of Justice," *Denver Post*, March 31, 2013. www.denverpost.com.

23. Quoted in Michael Radelet, "Capital Punishment in Colorado: 1859–1972," Office of the Colorado State Public Defender. http://pdweb.coloradodefenders.us.

24. Quoted in Michael Dow Burkhead, *A Life for a Life: The American Debate over the Death Penalty*. Jefferson, NC: McFarland, 2009, p. 118.

25. Quoted in Alaine Griffin, "Death Penalty: Those Who Lost Loved Ones Hold Divergent Views," *Hartford Courant*, April 4, 2012. http://articles.courant.com.

26. Quoted in ACLU.com, "Family Members of Murder Victims Speak Out Against Death Penalty," November 30, 2012. https://aclu-wa.org.

27. Quoted in ACLU.com, "Family Members of Murder Victims Speak Out Against Death Penalty."

28. Kathleen Garcia, "Death Penalty Hurts—Not Helps—Families of Murder Victims," *Nashua Telegraph*, March 28, 2010. www.nashuatelegraph.com.

29. Quoted in Burkhead, *A Life for a Life*, p. 118.

30. Amnesty International USA, "The Ultimate Denial of Human Rights." www.amnestyusa.org.

Chapter Three: Is the Risk of Executing an Innocent Person Too High?

31. Quoted in CNN.com, "After 15 Years on Death Row, Freedom," September 29, 2012. www.cnn.com.

32. Quoted in CNN.com, "After 15 Years on Death Row, Freedom."

33. Quoted in Josh Levs, "Innocent Man: How Inmate Michael Morton lost 25 Years of His Life," CNN.com, December 4, 2013. www.cnn.com.

34. Quoted in CBS News.com, "Record Number of Wrongful Convictions Overturned in 2013," February 4, 2014. www.cbsnews.com.

35. Quoted in Michael McLaughlin, "Carlos DeLuna Execution: Texas Put to Death an Innocent Man, Columbia University Team Says," *Huffington Post*, May 15, 2012. www.huffingtonpost.com.

36. Quoted in McLaughlin, "Carlos DeLuna Execution."

37. Quoted in McLaughlin, "Carlos DeLuna Execution."

38. Quoted in Gabrielle Levy, "Quinn's Difficult Decision Highlights Complicated Realities of Death Penalty Debate," *Medill Reports*, March 9, 2011. http://news.medill.northwestern.edu.

39. Quoted in Levy, "Quinn's Difficult Decision Highlights Complicated Realities of Death Penalty Debate."

40. Quoted in PR Newswire, "Texas Assessment Team Releases Report on State's Death Penalty System, Cites Urgent Need for Reform," September 18, 2013. www.prnewswire.com.

41. Quoted in Spencer S. Hsu, "Police Chiefs Lead Effort to Prevent Wrongful Convictions by Altering Investigative Practices," *Washington Post*, December 2, 2012. www.washington post.com.

42. Quoted in Hsu, "Police Chiefs Lead Effort to Prevent Wrongful Convictions by Altering Investigative Practices."

43. Quoted in Innocence Project, "New DNA Testing Reveals Innocence of Man on Florida's Death Row and Points to Victim's Daughter as Likely Perpetrator," May 13, 2013. www. innocenceproject.org.

Chapter Four: Is the Death Penalty Applied Unfairly?

44. Richard C. Dieter, "Struck by Lightning: The Continuing Arbitrariness of the Death Penalty Thirty-Five Years After Its Reinstatement in 1976," Death Penalty Information Center, July 2011. www.deathpenaltyinfo.org.

45. Quoted in Dieter, "Struck by Lightning."

46. Dieter, "Struck by Lightning."

47. Robert J. Smith, "The Geography of the Death Penalty and Its Ramifications," *Boston University Law Review*, August 22, 2011. www.deathpenaltyinfo.org.

48. Quoted in Adam Liptak, "Lawyers Stumble, and Clients Take Fall," *New York Times*, January 7, 2013. http://ideas.time.com.

49. Quoted in Touré, "Put to Death for Being Black: New Hope Against Judicial System Bias," *Time*, May 3, 2012.

50. Quoted in Death Penalty Information Center, "STUDIES: Jurors in Washington State More Likely to Impose Death on Black Defendants, 2014." www.deathpenaltyinfo.org.

51. Quoted in WRAL.com, "Study: Race Plays Role in N.C. Death Penalty," July 22, 2010. www.wral.com.

52. Quoted in Matt Smith, "'Racial Justice Act' Repealed in North Carolina," CNN.com, June 20, 2013. www.cnn.com.

53. Quoted in Kim Severson, "North Carolina Repeals Law Allowing Racial Bias Claim in Death Penalty Challenges," *New York Times*, June 5, 2013. www.nytimes.com.

54. Quoted in Severson, "North Carolina Repeals Law Allowing Racial Bias Claim in Death Penalty Challenges."

55. Quoted in John Bacon, "Washington Governor Suspends Death Penalty," *USA Today*, February 12, 2014. www.usato day.com.

56. Quoted in Bacon, "Washington Governor Suspends Death Penalty."

57. Quoted in Kelly Glista, "Judge: No Racial Bias in Death Penalty," *Hartford Courant*, October 12, 2013. http://articles.cou rant.com.

58. Quoted in Bacon, "Washington Governor Suspends Death Penalty."

Chapter Five: Are Death Penalty Methods Constitutional?

59. Quoted in Alan Johnson, "Inmate's Death Called 'Horrific' Under New, 2-Drug Execution," *Columbus Dispatch*, January 17, 2014. www.dispatch.com.

60. Quoted in Meredith Clark, "Family Says Execution Violated Inmate's 8th Amendment Rights," MSNBC.com, January 17, 2014. www.msnbc.com.

61. Quoted in Johnson, "Inmate's Death Called 'Horrific' Under New, 2-Drug Execution."

62. Quoted in American Civil Liberties Union, "The Case Against the Death Penalty," December 11, 2012. www.aclu.org.

63. Quoted in Tanya Lewis, "Why Lethal Injection Drugs Don't Always Work as Expected," LiveScience, May 1, 2014. www. huffingtonpost.com.

64. Quoted in Adam Liptak and Terry Aguayo, "After Problem Execution, Governor Bush Suspends the Death Penalty in Florida," *New York Times*, December 16, 2006. http://query. nytimes.com

65. Quoted in Larry Greenemeier, "Cruel and Usual? Is Capital Punishment by Lethal Injection Quick and Painless?," *Scientific American*, October 27, 2010. www.scientificamerican.com.

66. Quoted in Death Penalty Information Center, "New Revelations of Inmate's Struggles During Ohio Execution Attempt." www.deathpenaltyinfo.org.

67. Quoted in Nathan Koppel and Chris Herring, "Lethal Injection Draws Scrutiny in Some States," *Wall Street Journal*, October 15, 2009. http://online.wsj.com.

68. Quoted in Koppel and Herring, "Lethal Injection Draws Scrutiny in Some States."

69. Quoted in Andrew Welsh-Huggins, "Botched Execution Could Renew 'Cruel' Challenges," Yahoo.com, May 1, 2014. http://news.yahoo.com.

70. Quoted in Charlotte Alter, "Oklahoma Convict Who Felt 'Body Burning' Executed with Controversial Drug," *Time*, January 10, 2014. http://nation.time.com.

71. Quoted in Alter, "Oklahoma Convict Who Felt 'Body Burning' Executed with Controversial Drug."

72. Quoted in Josh Levs, Ed Payne, and Greg Botelho, "Oklahoma's Botched Lethal Injection Marks New Front in Battle over Executions," CNN.com, May 1, 2014. www.cnn.com.

73. Quoted in Koppel and Herring, "Lethal Injection Draws Scrutiny in Some States."

Related Organizations and Websites

American Civil Liberties Union (ACLU)
125 Broad St., 18th Floor
New York, NY 10004
phone: (212) 549-2500
fax: (212) 549-2646
website: www.aclu.org

The ACLU believes that capital punishment violates the Constitution's ban on cruel and unusual punishment. The ACLU Capital Punishment Project works to abolish the death penalty and its website provides information on death penalty issues.

Amnesty International USA
5 Penn Plaza, 16th Floor
New York, NY 10001
phone: (212) 807-8400
website: www.amnestyusa.org

Amnesty International is a worldwide movement of people who campaign for internationally recognized human rights. It tracks human rights abuses worldwide. Its website includes information about the use of the death penalty.

Campaign to End the Death Penalty (CEDP)
PO Box 25730
Chicago, IL 60625
phone: (773) 955-4841
website: www.nodeathpenalty.org

The CEDP is a national grassroots organization dedicated to the abolition of capital punishment in the United States. Its website has fact sheets about capital punishment and regular updates on death row cases.

Catholic Mobilizing Network (CMN)
3025 4th St. NE, Suite 118
Washington, DC 20017
phone: (202) 541-5290
website: http://catholicsmobilizing.org

CMN works to promote unconditional pro-life teaching and seeks to end the application of capital punishment. CMN works closely with Catholic, Protestant, interfaith, and secular organizations, along with universities and colleges, to promote dialogue and common action to abolish capital punishment.

Clark County Indiana Prosecuting Attorney
Steven D. Stewart
501 E. Court Ave.
215 County Government Bldg.
Jeffersonville, IN 47130
website: www.clarkprosecutor.org

This site from death penalty supporter Steven D. Stewart, prosecuting attorney in Clark County, Indiana, provides comprehensive information on the death penalty, including statistics, executions, laws, history, and over fifteen hundred death penalty links.

Criminal Justice Legal Foundation (CJLF)
2131 L St.
Sacramento, CA 95816
phone: (916) 446-3045
website: www.cjlf.org

The CJLF is a nonprofit, public interest law organization dedicated to achieving a balance between the rights of crime victims and the accused. The CJLF aims to assure that people who are guilty of committing crimes receive swift and certain punishment in an orderly and constitutional manner.

The Death Penalty Information Center (DPIC)
1101 Vermont Ave. NW, Suite 701
Washington, DC 20005
phone: (202) 289-2275
website: www.deathpenaltyinfo.org

The DPIC is a nonprofit organization that provides analysis and information on issues concerning capital punishment.

Equal Justice Initiative
122 Commerce St.
Montgomery, AL 36104
phone: (334) 269-1803
website: www.eji.org

The Equal Justice Initiative provides legal representation to indigent defendants and prisoners who have been denied fair and just treatment in the legal system.

Innocence Project
40 Worth St., Suite 701
New York, NY 10013
phone: (212) 364-5340
website: www.innocenceproject.org

The Innocence Project is dedicated to exonerating wrongfully convicted people through DNA testing and reforming the criminal justice system to prevent future injustice.

Justice for All
PO Box 55159
Houston, TX 77255
phone: (713) 935-9300
website: www.jfa.net; www.prodeathpenalty.com

Justice for All states that its mission is to act as an advocate for change in the criminal justice system to protect the lives and property of law-abiding citizens. It maintains a list and information about upcoming death row executions in Texas.

Murder Victims.com
website: www.murdervictims.com

This site provides resources for family and friends of murder victims, information on murder statistics, news, links, and a discussion forum.

National Center for Victims of Crime
200 M St. NW, Suite 480
Washington, DC 20036
phone: (202) 467-8700
website: www.ncvc.org

The National Center for Victims of Crime is the country's leading re-source for crime victims, including the families of murder victims. Its website provides links to pro–death penalty articles and resources.

National Coalition to Abolish the Death Penalty

1705 DeSales St. NW, 5th Floor
Washington, DC 20036
phone: (202) 331-4090
website: www.ncadp.org

The National Coalition to Abolish the Death Penalty is a collection of more than one hundred groups working together to stop executions in the United States and around the world.

Pro Death Penalty.com

website: www.prodeathpenalty.com

This site supports the death penalty and provides information on current death penalty issues, news items, links, articles, and other resources. It also provides case histories about scheduled and recent executions.

Students Against the Death Penalty

1600 Wickersham Ln., #3084
Austin, TX 78741
phone: (210) 601-7231
website: www.studentabolition.org

Students Against the Death Penalty works to end the death penalty through campaigns of public education and the promotion of youth activism.

Additional Reading

Books

Nicola Barber, *The Death Penalty*. New York: Rosen, 2012.

Robert M. Bohm, *Ultimate Sanction: Understanding the Death Penalty Through Its Many Voices and Many Sides*. New York: Kaplan, 2010.

Jenny Cromie and Lynn M. Zott, eds., *The Death Penalty*. Detroit: Greenhaven, 2011.

Syd Golston, *Death Penalty*. Farmington Hills, MI: Lucent, 2009.

Christine Watkins, ed., *The Ethics of Capital Punishment*. Detroit: Greenhaven, 2011.

Internet Sources

Amnesty International, "Death Penalty Facts," May 2012. www.amnestyusa.org/pdfs/DeathPenaltyFactsMay2012.pdf.

Death Penalty Information Center, "Facts About the Death Penalty," April 24, 2014. www.deathpenaltyinfo.org/documents/FactSheet.pdf.

Richard C. Dieter, "Struck by Lightning: The Continuing Arbitrariness of the Death Penalty Thirty-Five Years After Its Reinstatement in 1976," Death Penalty Information Center, July 2011. www.deathpenaltyinfo.org/documents/StruckByLightning.pdf.

Richard C. Dieter, "The 2% Death Penalty: How a Minority of Counties Produce Most Death Cases at Enormous Costs to

All," Death Penalty Information Center, October 2013. www .deathpenaltyinfo.org/documents/TwoPercentReport.pdf.

The Innocence Project, "DNA Exonerations Nationwide." www. innocenceproject.org/Content/DNA_Exonerations_Nation wide.php#.

Periodicals

John Bacon, "Washington Governor Suspends Death Penalty," *USA Today*, February 12, 2014. www.usatoday.com/story/ news/nation/2014/02/11/washington-death-penalty-ins lee/5394917.

Meredith Clark, "Is This the End for the Death Penalty?," MS-NBC.com, May 1, 2014. www.msnbc.com/msnbc/end-of-the -death-penalty.

Josh Levs, "Innocent Man: How Inmate Michael Morton Lost 25 Years of His Life," CNN.com, December 4, 2013. www. cnn.com/2013/12/04/justice/exonerated-prisoner-update -michael-morton.

Kim Severson, "Davis Is Executed in Georgia," *New York Times*, September 21, 2011. www.nytimes.com/2011/09/22/us/final -pleas-and-vigils-in-troy-davis-execution.html?pagewanted =all&_r=0.

Index

Note: Boldface page numbers indicate illustrations.

Picture Credits

About the Author

Carla Mooney is the author of many books for young adults and children. She lives in Pittsburgh, Pennsylvania, with her husband and three children.